Testimonials

This book showed me how I could change my own life and business for the better. The short anecdotes and stories easily helped me realize what was holding me back and gave me the tools for positive change. Shortly after reading this book, I felt the confidence to make the necessary changes I needed to take my business to the next level. This is the book I send to all my friends and business associates. I highly recommend this book!

Ian Franzen
Founder & President, College Web Pro Website
Development Company
New York, New York

Inspiring. Motivating. Enlightening. This book offers solid tips and strategies for letting go of past failures, overcoming obstacles, finding the courage to push past fear, and learning how to be disciplined in developing your strengths. Take Care of #1 So You Don't Step in #2 is a must-read for anyone looking to grow personally or professionally on their road to success.

Elisa Franzetta-Ware
Sr. Media Buyer, TCB
Innovative Communications
Pittsburgh, Pennsylvania

In ancient times, samurai lived by a code that cried victory and defeat are one in the same. Only by learning to live with defeat can you find victory. Loshelder teaches this concept beautifully. Developing unwavering courage and the willingness to take calculated risks is the only way to success and personal achievement. Learning comes from losing and winning comes from losing—a concept we all need to live by. Loshelder simply conveys the mutual welfare for all through the ideal of self-development and leadership. He says if everyone does his or her part, society will gain. Having a plan to make changes, using a process, and analyzing results is the keystone to success and fulfillment, and this is what Loshelder communicates so well. The journey is more important than the destination.

Gary Goltz, MBA
President, Goltz Healthcare Sales Strategies, Inc.
Los Angeles, California

David Loshelder provides insight into the importance of understanding yourself and the environment in order to achieve your goals. He creatively combines personal obstacles and achievements with key concepts that everyone could benefit from reading. I would highly recommend this book, not just as an inspirational read, but also for understanding the journey to success.

Rob Kalchthaler
Adult Services Librarian
Pittsburgh, Pennsylvania

This book needs to be on everyone's bookshelf, Kindle, or phone, ready to be read anywhere you go. I find passing time in between sitting at red lights and quickly reading a paragraph is a productive way to pick up the pieces of the success puzzle that this book provides. This is a book for everyone and for everywhere.

John Serbin
Three-Time USA National Judo Champion
San Jose, California

Dave's message to his readers is that success is a process, not a data point. It requires a balance of psychological, emotional, and physical commitment. Take the time to read this book and do the necessary self-reflection that will get you on the path you want to be.

Philip Farabaugh, MBA
Principal at Exodos
Pittsburgh, Pennsylvania

As a scientist in my day job and judo coach in my spare time not everything goes to plan. Experiments fail or give unexpected results and athletes under perform. But without an open mindset and the ability to self reflect we will never progress. David's book gives clear direction on how to approach these hurdles and move forward. As I say to my colleagues and students. Every day is a school day."

Iain H Reid BSc(Hons),MPhil
Senior Scientist, GlaxoSmithKline
UKCC Level 3 Judo Coach, Melbourn Judo Club
Stevenage, United Kingdom

Relatable, remarkable, and real! I loved what Dave had to say about commitment. In my mind, commitment was only about making a decision to do something you want and sticking to it. But it's actually more than that. There is a whole personal development to your commitment. Once you have committed, you still have to choose to better yourself each and every day, such as improving your skills, learning from others, keeping that fire alive in you that caused you to make the commitment in the first place. He explains this perfectly in his "10 Commandments to Commitment." Well worth the read!

Chasity Ross
Health and Fitness Coach
Kansas City, Missouri

Copyright © 2016 David Loshelder
All rights reserved. No part of this book may be reproduced or transmitted in any form or by any means, electronic or mechanical, including photocopying, recording, or by any information storage and retrieval system, without permission in writing from the author.

ISBN-10 0-9966883-7-4
ISBN-13 978-0-9966883-7-6
Cover design by D.V. Suresh
Illustration by Deborah Alexander
Freeze Time Media

Quantity Sales Discounts
Take Care of #1 So You Don't Step In #2 is available at significant quantity discounts when purchased in bulk for clients gifts, sales promotions, and premiums. For details and discount information for print format,contact *Dave@take-careofnumberone.com*, tel. (412) 290-6955 or *http://www.takecareofnumberone.com*.

TAKE CARE
OF
#1
SO YOU DON'T STEP IN #2

7 WAYS TO
MANAGE YOURSELF
SO YOU CAN
EFFECTIVELY
LEAD OTHERS

TAKE CARE
OF
#1
SO YOU DON'T
STEP IN #2

7 WAYS TO
MANAGE YOURSELF
SO YOU CAN
EFFECTIVELY
LEAD OTHERS

David Loshelder

To Nathan, Jacob, and Noah

Acknowledgments

This book was made possible by the support and encouragement of the following people:

My wife, Jennifer, and my three children, Nathan, Jacob, and Noah, whose love is manifested in so many ways, but particularly in their generous patience, support, and understanding. A special thanks goes to the following people who helped with the creation of this book: JJ McKeever, Shawn Deffner, Helen Auman, Dr. Marisa Pedulla, and Pam Greer; my publisher, Di Freeze, whose suggestions and creativity made this book a published work for all to read; and the list continues with the people that were a great influence and offered so much to this book … and to anyone who strives to be a champion and a leader.

Contents

Introduction xvii

Part 1 1

Your Wake Up-Call: What Makes You Act the Way You Do? 1

Chapter 1 3

Stop Being the Puppet in Someone's Puppet Show 3
    May the Force be with You 8

Chapter 2 17

Three Things That are Keeping You from Succeeding 17
    1. Gravitational Pull: You 17
    2. Gravitational Pull: People 20
    3. Gravitational Pull: Environment 22

Chapter 3 25

It is Just Not Worth Focusing on the Two Percent! 25
    Is Your Cup Half Empty or Half Full? 29

Chapter 4 31

Five Obstacles You Will Need to Jump Over to Get What You Want in Life 31
    Obstacle #1 31
    Fear: Being Afraid Does Not Mean You are Fearful 31
    Obstacle #2 37

You Have a Serious Dilemma: Good Things Turning Bad 37
Obstacle #3..40
Ask Yourself, Why am I Doing This?.....................................40
Obstacle #4..45
I'm Helpless: Who Do I Blame Now?....................................45
Obstacle #5..49
Walking the Tightrope of Life and Keeping Your Balance 49

Part 2 53

The Building Blocks to Your Success.......................................53

Chapter 5..55

Play to Win...55

Chapter 6..61

Increasing Your Expectations Beyond What You Think is Reasonable..61

Chapter 7..69

The Champion's Trio: Scoring a Hat-Trick in Life...................69
 #1 Criticism: Who Really Cares What Others Say.............70
 #2 Failure is Not an Option..75
 #3 Staying Composed in the Face of Adversity..................81

Chapter 8..83

Building Internal Strength...83
 Attitude: Your Attitude is Not Everything; It is the Only

Thing...83
Perseverance: The Hard Work After Doing the Hard Work
....86
Discipline: Remember, Discipline Weighs Ounces, While
Regret Weighs Tons...88
Momentum: Making Your Life Work for You..........94

Chapter 9...97

Shut Up and Get to the Gym..97
Taking Action..97
How to Become Stronger, Better, Faster....................99
I Cannot Concentrate on Anything!..........................101

Chapter 10...105

If at First You Don't Succeed, Don't Come Back Home....105
Winners Expect to Get Hit and They Like It...........107

Part 3..109

Putting it all Together and Coming out on Top.........109

Chapter 11..111

The Seven Things You Should do Every Day 111

Chapter 12...115

Commitment: You are Either in or You are Out.........115
The Commitment Highway..116
A Little Secret to Commitment: Do not Quit!..........124

Chapter 13...127

- Goals: Being Better than You Were Yesterday ... 127
  - You Cannot Manage What You do not Measure ... 130
  - No, Seriously, What Are Goals? ... 132
  - Look at Those Goals Again! ... 139
  - Goals: A Journey or a Destination? ... 145

Chapter 14 ... 149

Focus: The Only Way to Set Your Life on Fire ... 149

Chapter 15 ... 155

Self-Talk: The Best Way to Motivate Yourself to Do Anything! ... 155

Chapter 16 ... 161

Vision: Seeing to Believing to Creating ... 161

Chapter 17 ... 165

Mental Rehearsal: Making Your Dreams a Reality ... 165

Chapter 18 ... 171

Simulation: Planning, Practice, Patience Makes Perfect ... 171

Chapter 19 ... 177

Living in the Zone ... 177
  - Giving Back to Others ... 185

Introduction

Frustration. Have you ever felt frustration to the point that it caused so much anger that you could not endure it one more day? Have you ever set a goal, worked as hard as you could, only to fall short of that goal time and time again? This happened to me and it totally sucked. To be honest, for five straight years, gold was not in my color scheme. I simply hated it, and, frankly, I am still bummed out about it. Yeah, I know what you are saying: get over it and move on. I think you deserve an explanation. Let me tell you how gold evaded me time and time again.

The year was 1979. This is the year my father enrolled me in my first judo class. I loved it and could not wait for the next practice. I practiced, read books, watched videos, and participated in competitions. Judo became my obsession — an obsession that led me to win first place in most of the competitions I entered. At the mere age of twelve, my coach encouraged me to compete at the U.S. Nationals in Decatur, Illinois, in the eleven- and twelve-year-old division. I was a big shot around the Pittsburgh area, and I thought this would be an easy sweep. I had visions of proudly standing atop the podium donning the color of a true champion, the color of gold. I suffered defeat quite easily that day in my first two matches and walked home empty handed. I learned that it was too easy to go from hero to zero.

The next year, I was determined to improve my skills. When nationals came around in 1983, I was ready for the challenge. The Junior Olympic Nationals were held in Dayton, Ohio, and with another year of training under my belt, I was determined to win this one. So many times, in my own mind, I envisioned myself a national champion. National champion had such a nice ring to it, and this would finally be my chance. I had attained the rank of purple belt (two belt ranks from black belt). The rank was appropriate for someone of my age and skill level, but I really did not care about the color of my belt. The only color I cared about was gold. Gold would earn me the bragging rights of being one of the nation's best.

When I arrived in Dayton, the air was thick with enthusiasm and excitement. I eagerly awaited my first match, and after a brief introduction from the tournament director, the competition began. I competed in the opening match, which proved to be experience against strength. My foe was a formidable opponent, an aggressive kid with good attacks and a strong grip. We both fought hard for about two minutes before I was able to finish the match out with a submission hold and win convincingly. The feeling I had was not of joy, but of relief. I thought, "One down, several to go."

My next match was against a boy who had more experience and skill. He was a short, stubby kid with dark brown hair. He was muscular for a kid his age. You know the kind of kid who always seems angry about something? He was like that. He probably wanted the same thing I wanted, and maybe just as badly, even though I doubted that anyone could want to win a national championship as much as I did. Nonetheless, he looked like a tall order, and when we squared off, he had the upper hand for about forty seconds. I decided I had better step up my game and get this job done as quickly as I could, so I put it in high gear and started to work him, knocking him down several times. I felt a shift in momentum, which gave me the upper hand and control of the match. I accumulated several points during the match and won it, which positioned me in the finals, just where I wanted to be.

You know how life has a way of throwing you a curveball? My curveball was last year's national champion. I was new to the national scene and was not familiar with all the competitors. Apparently, he was a known entity, according to the kid I sat next to after my second match. My new confidant's name was Ray.

I sat down next to Ray, whom I had met that day in warm-ups before the tournament began.

"Nice match," he offered. "You look good out there."

"Thanks," I said. "He was a tough one. Glad I got through it."

"Yeah, and I see you got 'the man' for your next match," Ray said.

"And so?" I asked.

"Oh, he schooled me last year. I really didn't do much in that match. Really, it didn't last that long. He grabbed me and tossed me, and it was over. I was done at that point, and my dad and I went home," Ray replied.

"He beat you that easily?" I asked, somewhat astonished.

"I don't think he broke a sweat. It was that quick," Ray said.

As Ray explained how "the man" easily dispensed of him, we proceeded to watch his first match, and Ray mentioned how he demonstrated a true "workmanlike" performance as he disposed of his opponent with ease and grace. He dumped the kid he was fighting and tangled him up in the tightest hold I had ever seen. The poor kid was so tied up that he could not move or breathe. "The man" won the match convincingly, and since he and I won our preliminary matches, this positioned us to meet in the next round—the final round—the gold medal round!

Did you ever get that feeling that something was not right or something bad was going to happen just before it did? As it turned out, "the man" gripped me, disappeared under my legs, tossed me over, and pinned me flat on the mat. I never really went against anyone with his skill before, so it was a foreign experience to me, to say the least.

I was out of the running for the national prize, and the dream of my national championship was still just a dream. I dusted off my uniform, and my pride, and picked up my silver medal. Silver is silver; it is not gold. You cannot call yourself a national champion if you take second place. If you had asked me if I was happy with my performance, I would have said, "Yes." Was I satisfied? No! See, I wanted to say I was a national champion. Saying I took second was not good enough.

As the years passed, I competed in many tournaments, winning most of them. However, those national events were my nemesis. Every year in the junior events, I fell short and received second or third place. When I reached the senior men's division, I started to compete at this level; my desperate pursuit for the national title remained unchanged. I really believed I had a great chance my first year in the men's division.

It was 1990, in San Diego, California. I lost in the quarterfinals, fought back by winning several matches in the consolation rounds, and won a bronze medal, third best in the country. In 1991, I was in Honolulu, Hawaii. I fought very hard and won most of my matches. Unfortunately, I lost a key one and walked away with a bronze medal, third best in the country ... again. In 1992, in my hometown of Pittsburgh, Pennsylvania, I readied myself, got myself in great shape, and primed myself to win this one.

Let me spare you the details on this one. You guessed it; I once again won the bronze medal and was third best in the country. In 1993, this time in Indianapolis, Indiana, I lost the gold medal and walked away with the bronze medal and third best in the country. Since I was getting older, I recognized I was running out of time to win that gold. I was twenty-four years old, entering graduate school, and my focus was shifting to my education and career development. My hours of training and traveling slowly declined, along with my dream of winning a gold medal.

I decided to give it one more shot in 1994. The U.S. Nationals were held in Irvine, California, a mere five-hour flight to the Golden State. This was my last chance to secure the gold medal I had worked toward for so many years. I was not only in the best shape possible, but I was also ready for battle. Since I was getting older, I decided to move up a weight class. It was becoming more difficult to make the lower weight class at which I had competed for so many years. I fought hard and performed better than I had in many years against the nation's best. I beat everyone easily, and then I met the former national champion in this weight class. It did not matter to me that he was last year's world champion. I fought as hard and as smart as I knew how. It was a great match and a fun one to watch, according to those who cheered us on. I thought that if I beat him, it would then be a cakewalk to the finals. Well, I did not win. It was very close, but I did not come up with the goods. I walked away with the bronze for the fifth time in a row!

In retrospect, even though I did not win, I felt proud of my performance because I left everything on the table and was in the "zone." Everything seemed to flow, and it was so much fun! That is the point of competing, right? You want to have fun. That is why we do it.

Yes, I was the third best in the nation that year too. You might think by this point that I went to a corner of the gym, dripping with disappointment. The funny thing was that I did not feel that bad. I was disappointed, of course, but not devastated. I realized that I gave it everything I had, and I did have success, but it was this very last match of my career where I found what it meant to compete. It was the feeling of being in the moment, where the past meets the future, where your skill level meets the challenge. This state of mind regarding experiences is what famous psychologist Mihaly Csikszentmihalyi called "flow," or as we refer to it, "being in the zone." This is where I was and enjoyed every moment of it. At this point, it was not about winning, but about performing and feeling the performance. The effortless flow I felt was exhilarating.

This is really the thesis of this book. We all have goals. If you set your goals high and lofty, but fall short of them, in actuality you have not lost anything. In fact, you have gained from setting those goals and trying desperately to reach them. The ups and downs of the journey form the experience, not the end goal. Pulling yourself through the agony of defeat can either destroy you or define you. You have the choice. It is about the journey, not the destination.

Through all of my observations and years of working with people, I found there are three divisions of life that affect the outcomes. I divided this book into three parts. Part 1 of this book is the Wake-Up Call section. Many of the problems you may face stem from a lack of awareness as to what influences them. This section will help you examine the basic habitual patterns and the internal and external psychological conditions that negatively affect you. Once you become aware of the limiting factors that consciously and unconsciously affect your behaviors, you will move to Part 2: Break Ground and Start Digging.

Part 2 dives into the psychological structure and perspective that is necessary to reach the level of success you desire and deserve. These are the building blocks that you need for your success. You cannot build a house on a weak foundation. Actually, you can, but the house will eventually fall down. Without a strong psychological and physical structure, you cannot build your success. This section will give you the tools and perspectives to establish a strong foundation that you can build upon to move to Part 3 of this book.

Once you become aware, break down the barriers, and understand what is limiting you in Part 1, you can then start to build a strong psychological and physical foundation that provides you the opportunity to "Build the house of success." Part 3 is the culmination of successful principles to which world-class athletes, business professionals, great students, and anyone who consistently works and performs at the highest level adhere to. This part of the book is where the rubber meets the road. The people who mastered these skills and applied them on a consistent basis have demonstrated outstanding results. The great thing about these skills is that they are not only for the Olympic athlete, but also for anyone to master, including you. Make no mistake about it; this is a journey, not a destination. You will need to constantly revisit, tweak, adjust, and practice these concepts. Coming back to this book time and time again will be important to help you stay on track. So let us dive in now and start this journey!

PART 1

Your Wake Up-Call: What Makes You Act the Way You Do?

CHAPTER 1

Stop Being the Puppet in Someone's Puppet Show

I had always subscribed to the notion that if I won the "big one," I was the best. Later in my career, I realized that maybe I would have been the best on that day, but, if that day was played over a hundred times, there would have been many winners, statistically speaking. However, I did not win that day and that is the point. When you give everything you have, practice the best you know how, train hard and play hard, you do not play for the moment, you play for a lifetime. You build skills, experiences, and knowledge every time you put yourself through the paces. There are no guarantees that you will win a competition; however, it is up to you to define "winning." Each time you set a goal with the realization that the end result may be excruciating heartache, you help yourself become stronger, smarter, better, more skilled, more capable, more able, and more confident. In essence, you are not playing for that day; you are playing for a lifetime. You are also playing not just for yourself, but for others. When you strive to be the best in whatever endeavor you choose, you may initially think it is for your own selfish claims, but in reality, you build those skills for the benefit of others. All of your personal trials and tribulations make you a better, more capable person. This allows you to do the most marvelous thing you can do and give back to everyone you know or want to know. The beauty of this is that you alone do not benefit from all your hard work. As you build your skills, your family, children, friends, coworkers, community, and even the nation, can benefit from what you put yourself through. You see this in nature all the time. Take a look at the honeybee.

When the honeybee moves from flower to flower collecting nectar, there are benefits for both the honeybee *and* the flower. To understand how this works, we will look at the flower first. Every flower has two different parts—the stamens and the pistil, or male and female parts. Stamens produce pollen, and pollen pollinates the pistil. Only when this happens will a fruit grow from the base of the flower. This is where the honeybee comes into help. The foraging honeybee will collect the pollen and carry it on their legs. When a honeybee visits many different flowers in a single trip, that pollen brushes against the pistils and pollination takes place. This transfer of pollen ensures the flower is able to reproduce the next generation, thanks to the hard work of the honeybee.

You might be asking: How does a honeybee relate to me? If you extrapolate this analogy, you will see that the honeybee is working hard to collect honey for itself and the colony, but a collateral consequence occurs when it moves from flower to flower, continually transferring the pollen and the genetic code to other flowers. The honeybee's skills and actions are literally "rubbing off" on the flower, ensuring future flowers propagate and flourish. This is no different when you set goals, work hard to achieve them, and subsequently build the skills necessary to be successful.

One person's goals affect the lives of many. As you embark on the journey to meet your goals, you unknowingly pick up skills that may impact others as much as they do you. You affect others just as the pollen fertilizes the other flowers helping them reproduce. You "rub off on" others just by being the person you become when you build skills and talents. *Striving for a goal is not a selfish endeavor; it is a benevolent action.*

When you look back at life, you will find that all your goals, even the ones that you did not reach, affected you in ways that you did not even realize. These new skills, new knowledge, and new abilities will be transferred to others in positive ways that will make a difference in their lives. When you work hard for something and stay focused on the process, you will realize that you have gathered much along the way, just like a honeybee collecting pollen on its hind legs. The bee has no idea it is passing the genes of one flower to the next, helping generations of flowers produce more flower and more fruit. It is focused on one goal—to collect nectar for itself and the colony. When this happens, nature is structured to share its benefits unselfishly, and it is no different for you.

Consider this: You are working hard to achieve a goal and the mere action you exert toward that goal is making you bigger and stronger, physically, intellectually, emotionally, and spiritually, even if you never reach the goal! *The process of striving is more important than arriving.* So, why not try anything you want! You never really fail at anything if you try, right? With this perspective, you cannot lose.

Here is the kicker. You will inevitably share this with others; however, you must start with yourself. You must rid yourself of self-delusion, banish doubt, and limit self-imposed worries of failure. This is why I am writing this book. If I can communicate my message to you, and you benefit from it, then all of my bronze medals will have paid off tenfold.

Over the years, along with the national medals, I picked up several silver medals in international competitions. Because of this, I accumulated so many competition points that the U.S. ranking body listed me as ranked number one in my weight class for two of those years, even though I never actually won a national title. Since I was so consistent, I was considered number one in my weight class, but what was the point? I thought about this for quite a while but always came up with the old phrase, "The sum of the parts is greater than the whole." What do I mean by this? The premise is that you need certain skills, concepts, and ideas to produce results in life. It is not just the end result, but also the quality of each result that makes a difference. If you put all of those ideas together and mash, mix, grind, and stir them up, then you will have more of you to offer than when you started. This gives you not only more of what you want, but more of what you can give others. This is the point! You have to take care of number one (you) first before you can do anything else.

There are three bad things that can happen if you do not take care of number one. First, if you do not take care of your health by eating well and exercising, you will gain unwanted pounds. Your cholesterol and blood lipids go up to dangerous unhealthy levels, and one day you have a heart attack. That is bad. The second thing is that if you do not take care of your brain and keep learning, you become intellectually stunted. Lastly, if you do not take care of your money, you will be without it. If you believe your life could be better now, just think how much worse it could be if you were ill, thoughtless, and penniless. That is about as bad as it gets.

Why do some people continually succeed and others do not? What do Olympic athletes, astronauts, and CEOs have in common? Are you unable to perform at your best or push yourself past your expectations when it really counts? Is your career stagnated? Are you dieting and having difficulty losing the last few pounds, or worse, not even staying on the diet? Are you a student who is unable to earn the grades you are capable of achieving?

Imagine if you had everything you wanted. Stop and think about it. Everything. What would that be like? You would wake up in the morning and come downstairs to your coffee and eggs and bacon cooked just the way you like them and ready to eat. You continue with your day and everything goes perfectly for you. Everything falls into place and nothing ever goes wrong. This continues day after day. That would be nice.

Obviously, that is not reality. In reality, some things work out and some things do not. A good friend of mine would always say to me, "Some things are easy and some things are hard. Some things move slowly, some things move fast." This is superficially profound, to be sure. In this book, I am going to look at the seemingly unpredictable and uncontrollable parts of life. You will learn that with a little effort and planning, the unpredictable(s) and uncontrollable(s) can be predicted, controlled, managed, and obtained.

May the Force be with You

Mr. Gorbachev, tear down this wall!
—Ronald Reagan

In 1977, when I was seven years old, one of my all-time favorite movies premiered. It was *Star Wars*. It became a worldwide pop culture favorite that is going strong to this day, with more sequels to come. Even now, I can remember the legendary Jedi Knight Obi-Wan Kenobi saying to the young Jedi Knight Luke Skywalker, "May the Force be with you," just before Skywalker embarked on the mission to destroy the Death Star and the Dark Side of the force.

Since that day, I think about the forces at play in my life, the good and bad forces that are always there. This was one of the overarching themes of this movie, as I remember it. Not a bad philosophy to live by, I would say. Similarly, in any life situation, there is a protagonist and an antagonist. The Chinese call it yin and yang. We call it good and bad. In physics, scientists study gravity and anti-gravity, two forces competing to pull you forward or push you away. Without active and purposeful resistance, the gravity of life simply takes over. It is constantly tugging at you. If you do not fight it, it will drag you down and pull you away from what you want or where you want to go and be. If you actively fight it, resist it, and are determined to succeed, you will find yourself climbing the hill of success.

Kurt Lewin coined a phrase for this phenomenon, referring to it as "Force Field Analysis." The Force Field Analysis has influenced many professional fields, particularly in the social sciences and change-management processes. Lewin explained that whenever driving forces are stronger than restraining forces, the status quo or equilibrium changes. Lewin wrote, "An issue is held in balance by the interaction of two opposing sets of forces—those seeking to promote change (driving forces) and those attempting to maintain the status quo (restraining forces)." The concept of Force Field Analysis provides a framework that demonstrates how opposing forces influence a situation. The driving forces (positive) help you move toward your goal and restraining (negative) forces block you from achieving it. These two forces are always in play and are always present whether you like it or not.

For change to happen, according to Lewin, the positive force must upset the status quo or equilibrium by adding favorable conditions or reducing the resistant forces. Whether it is your behavior, a group, a business, or an organization, these forces will push you in a positive direction or negative direction, depending on the strength of the two influences. So this begs the question: How can you beat the negative forces so they do not impede your efforts?

The first step is to be mindful that negative influences are present. The second is to recognize these negative forces that are influencing you at some level. The third is to make an analysis of which negative factors are influencing your behavior and the potential consequences or outcomes. Ask yourself: How is the force affecting me? What am I doing differently now than before? Am I moving toward my goals or away from them? After you have answered those three questions, start to identify the three possible fields of application for the Force Field Analysis:

1. Investigation of the balance of power of a certain situation/issue;
2. Identification of the most relevant stakeholders and target groups for a certain initiative;
3. Identification of both competitors and alliance partners and how each target group can be influenced.

These forces are present at all times. By using a model like Lewin's Force Field Analysis, you will be able to uncover many of life's influences. However, an analysis will only take you so far. Once you have analyzed it all, you must adopt the attitude of a winner to use it to overcome what is stopping you.

Let us look at a problem that more than sixty percent of the American population is dealing with: obesity. Many Americans say they are on a diet. Statistics show that people who lose weight usually gain it back along with a few extra pounds. The other problem is that some people start a diet and simply cannot stay with it, and as a result, they never lose any weight. This sense of failure and disgust perpetuates the downward spiral to their self-esteem and deepens their depression. Finally, in their most vulnerable state of weakness, hunger makes them reach for the glazed donut once again, destroying all hopes of that thin waistline. That is depressing. What is so hard about losing five, ten, or fifteen pounds in the first place? What is hindering their motivation? What makes them give up? Why is their willpower affected so easily when it comes to eating a well-balanced meal and a few less calories? Well, one way is to use the model of the Force Field Analysis. It helps identify some of the forces that may prevent someone from slimming down into that smaller bathing suit.

Let me take you through an example of a man named John who lost and gained hundreds of pounds in his life. John, age forty-seven, comes in at around two hundred twenty pounds. He has a forty-inch waistline and is five feet eight inches tall. As John always said, "Being of short stature and two hundred twenty pounds places me in the 'I'm not overweight, I'm just six inches too short' category." John has embarked on numerous weight loss ventures and has failed. Like many others who lost pounds in the past, John was the one who gained it back and then some. Over the years, he just got heavier, causing more health problems as the years went on.

What was his problem? He obviously had an effective way to lose the weight. Nevertheless, at some point, he went back to his old eating habits and put the weight back on. However, this did change, or I should say, he changed. John said, "I made changes in what I chose to eat, how I exercised and introduced other lifestyle changes, but I did not realize what was influencing me. Since I did not know what was pushing me over that cliff, I couldn't push back to stop myself from falling over." Only after an intensive self-analysis did John lose the weight and keep it off.

Initially, he did not have an awareness of the root causes of his problem. Success came when he used the Force Field Analysis model to help him understand what forces were working against him and which forces were working for him. Once he honestly and objectively evaluated them, John could then make a plan and lifestyle changes that he would stick to in order to lose the weight and keep it off. I will look at John's analysis to see how he identified the forces that were influencing his behavior.

First, John investigated the balance of influence that stopped him from keeping the weight off. As he looked at it, he realized that there were several factors: time, resources, knowledge, low self-esteem, and bad habits.

Step 1: Investigate and Identify

1. John investigated the balance of influence of his issue.
    - Time, resources, knowledge, low self-esteem
2. John identified target groups for a certain weight loss initiative.
    - John, nutritionist, doctor, family, fitness trainer
3. John identified both competitors and alliance partners and how each target group can be influenced.
    - Time, family, kids, activity schedule, work schedule

Step 2: Implement a Force Field Analysis

1. John defined the change issue by describing the current and the desired situation.
    - The current issue is that John falls in the overweight category and is emotionally and physically unhealthy.
    - The desired state is that John would like to weigh one hundred fifty pounds and be healthier, happier, and more physically able.
2. John then constructed a Force Field Diagram that

detailed (1) the problem, (2) the desired state, (3) the driving forces, (4) the restraining forces, and (5) scored each force field rating from 1 (weak) to 6 (strong).

3. John added the scores on each side to see where the division of strength lay for driving force and the restraining force (see Figure 1).

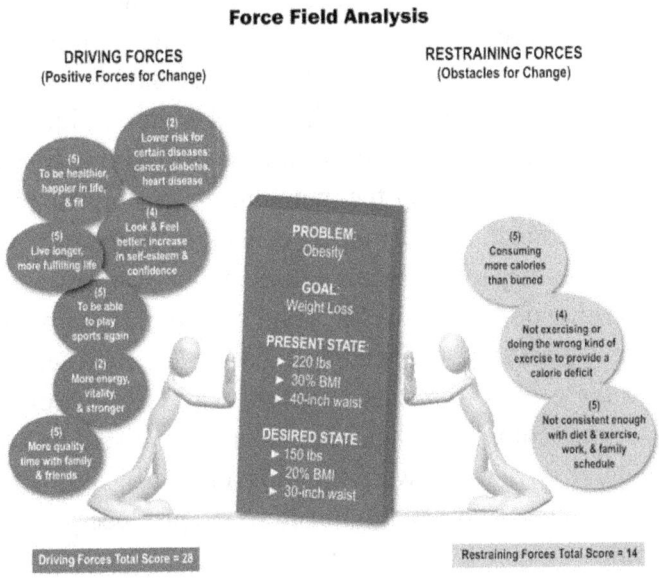

As he reviewed the Force Field Analysis, he found he developed a compelling case for change. In Figure 1, John tallied the scores from both sides of the Force Field ledger. He found the driving forces outweighed the restraining forces two to one. The driving forces totaled a score of twenty-eight, while the restraining forces totaled half that at fourteen. Since the positive forces for change doubled the negative forces, this gave John much more hope, possibility, and motivation to move forward with his plan. Now he could focus on what pushes him instead of what was pulling him away from the goal. Also, by weighing each one, this gave him the ability to prioritize what was most important to him, therefore making it much easier for him to design a plan of action. For John, the driving and restraining forces were both valid, but likewise, both elements of both forces could be changed and regulated. The primary driving forces were John consuming too many calories and not staying consistent with his diet and exercising mainly because of his hectic schedule. Assigning a score of five (strong force) for the two restraining forces, he was able to identify the main obstacles to overcome.

Of course, not participating in the appropriate exercise necessary to produce a calorie deficit was also rated as another obstacle to tackle. John's dilemma determined what needed to be changed first. Eating less food seemed like the easiest and most efficient way to lose weight. Far more complicated was squeezing exercise time into his busy day. These were the most critically significant forces that would need to be altered to produce positive results.

The first step is assessing the situation. Now it is your turn. Below are seventeen questions to help you effectively design your own Force Field Analysis. If it is a personal issue or a problem you are having in your business, these seventeen questions can help you start to analyze the problem and help you design a plan of action to produce positive changes.

Steps for Implementing a Force Field Analysis and Summary Questions:

1. Investigate the balance of influence of his issue
2. Identify the issues and target groups for a certain initiative
3. Identify both competitors and alliance partners and how each target group can be influenced
4. Start with a well-defined change issue to be discussed by describing the current and the desired situation.
   - Current issue is that John falls in the overweight category
5. Draw a Force Field Diagram.
6. Are the driving and restraining forces valid?
7. Can they be changed?
8. Which are the most critical ones?
9. How significant is each single force?
10. Which ones can be altered, and which cannot?
11. How long will it take to modify some of the forces?
12. Which forces, if altered, would produce rapid change?
13. Which skills are necessary to modify some forces and are they available?
14. Elaborate and list the driving and restraining forces and allocate them to the respective columns.
15. Allocate a score to each force, using a numerical scale.
16. Calculate the total score for both columns: the driving and restraining forces.

17. Determine whether a change is feasible.

Making this in-depth assessment was the first step to understanding the forces that were stopping John from losing the weight and keeping it off. Now it is your turn to identify what forces are for you and what forces are against you.

CHAPTER 2

Three Things That are Keeping You from Succeeding

There are lots of things that are beyond our control. Fortunately, character is different. That's completely within our control. The poor and the rich, the slow and the smart, the plain and the pretty all have an equal opportunity to become people of character.
—Michael Josephson

1. Gravitational Pull: You

You pull yourself down by the beliefs you hold and what you say to yourself. These self-imposed limits create a ceiling for your potential. When you place a ceiling on your own potential, you are unlikely to attempt anything more than you are already doing. When you are mired in comfort, there is no pressure to move. Examples of this type of gravitational pull are bad habits and routines that no longer serve a purpose.

If you think about gravity as physicists do, the more mass an object has, the heavier it is, and the more gravity it has on other objects. Have you ever "pulled yourself down" by thinking that you were not capable, could not complete a certain task, get a promotion, and consequently felt like a real dunce? Most of you have experienced this at one time or another. This mindset is your own gravitational pull, which holds you back from taking chances and risking failure.

Let me take this analogy further and illustrate the danger of having too much of a gravitational pull that could make recovery impossible. Our friends in the physics department say that in the universe, stars that are twenty times larger than our sun go through a process at the end of their lives in which they eventually collapse and form black holes. Stars continuously fuse lighter elements into heavier ones during their lifetime. During the process of fusion, there is a constant inward pull due to gravity and outward push due to pressure, such that the two balance each other. If a star is massive enough, it will fuse elements into iron. As more energy goes into fusing iron than is produced, this is the end of the line, and the star runs out of fuel. Gravity wins the battle against pressure, causing the core to collapse under its own weight. At this point, the star's outer layers explode in an extremely violent supernova. When such a core is more than two and a half times as massive as the sun, the inward pull of gravity is so immense that the core continues collapsing upon it, resulting in the formation of a "black hole." When a black hole is created, the gravity is so immense that even light cannot escape, hence the name "black hole."

This analogy has psychic parallels to how we single-handedly destroy our motivation and belief in ourselves. If you play this out and compare how a star collapses due to energy depletion and how we can eventually collapse psychologically, there are stark similarities. Let me provide the parallel.

First, we shall examine the star that starts to fuse lighter elements to heavier ones. This is no different from when you start to make small, irritating problems fuse in your mind, making them larger and heavier than they really are. It is the old adage, "making a mountain out of a mole hill," right? Second, there is a constant inward pull due to gravity and outward push due to pressure, such that the two balance each other and pressure starts to build. You build up pressure just as the star does. These feelings become more and more intense, and you find yourself becoming frustrated and angry. At this point, your rational thinking is affected and becomes unclear. Now, in keeping with the supernova example, if the pressure is great enough and the star big enough, then the elements fuse to make iron and the fusion process ends. The star runs out of energy. For you, this is where the pressure within you becomes so great that you shut down and you stop thinking. For the star, gravity wins the battle against the pressure; the core collapses under its own weight and the star's outer layers erupt in a supernova. When the gravity of life takes you to the edge, you implode and explode in some manner. At this point in the life of a star, a black hole forms where light cannot escape. Your black hole is when you feel hopeless and depressed, unmotivated, and unwilling to try. All of this is within your mind and can be reversed.

Translation: Do not let your own inward pull of gravity, your self-doubt, fear, or lack of ambition lead you into your own black hole. Do not let your own psychic gravity get the best of you. It is all within your will to overcome it.

2. Gravitational Pull: People

We judge ourselves by what we feel capable of doing, while others judge us by what we have already done.
—Henry Wadsworth Longfellow

Think about the people who care about you. When considering a new endeavor, you may hear whispers and warnings of "You can't do it." Perhaps in an effort to prevent you from failing and the accompanying humiliation, they caringly suggest that "You shouldn't do it." They could also snidely ask, "Why would you want to do that?" Whatever words or phrases they employ, they are telling you, "Why try, you won't succeed at this anyway." Have you ever had this experience? I sure have.

These people care about you! They're looking out for your best interests. They do not want you to get hurt or fail. Since they do not want you to fail (possibly resulting in them feeling bad as well), they tell you not to try. If you do not try, you will not fail and no one gets hurt! Logical, right? These statements and suggestions are so powerful that it is like having a professional hypnotist around you and providing suggestive statements all day long.

It is disheartening to realize this attitude pervades the lives of so many. You might say, "Not me. I think for myself. I do not let others dictate my beliefs or drive my dreams." Perhaps if you live alone, buddy up to the television, avoid the workplace, and merely stay at home staring at walls, you can think what you want to think and hypnotize yourself in any way you choose.

Of course, I am not a hypnotist, but even my words are providing suggestions and making you more aware of the influences in your life. You will encounter many people who influence your life in some fashion, for better or worse. If you are hanging out with the wrong people who do not support what you want do in life, they will attempt to guide you in a negative way. You may not even recognize what they are doing or understand why until it is too late and an opportunity to win the game has passed.

Like viruses, behaviors and attitudes are contagious. If you are around people who are coughing, sneezing, and have a runny nose, there is a good chance you will pick up the same common cold they have. I guess that is why doctors call it a common cold, because it is so common. When you associate with people who are not aligned with your vision and goals, or worse, surreptitiously influence your mind and behaviors, you may be inclined to start acting like they act, or believing what they believe. You pick up certain patterns of behavior and find yourself spending time in the wrong places at the wrong times.

Nature provides a number of examples of this phenomenon. A case in point is the zombie ant. As it turns out, some ants that live in the rainforest venture from the high tops of the trees at night. In doing so, some encounter a fungus that attaches itself to the ant and burrows into its body. It makes its way to the ant's brain, controls the ant's behavior, and convinces it to stagger away from the ant colony. The ant eventually climbs up a tree, attaches itself to a branch using its pinchers, and dies. After this happens, the fungi uses enzymes to break down the ant's hard exoskeleton and eerily grows out and up from its head. This graphic analogy should say something about the nature of those with whom you hang out.

Yikes! Is it really that bad? Are your questionable acquaintances prepared to take over your body with their intrusive thoughts, crowding your head like fungi? I would argue that this is indeed what is happening (minus your head exploding and fungi growing upward from your skull). These people are using any means possible, such as ideologies, persuasions, propaganda, and good old-fashioned goading to influence you. Now, if that does not feel like fungi saturating your poor brain, I do not know what is. What you watch on television, what you read, the music you listen to, the people you associate with, and virtually anything that infiltrates your consciousness may affect your psyche, thoughts, beliefs, and behaviors, if you let them!

3. Gravitational Pull: Environment

Of course, you frequently face situations over which you have little to no control. This happens in everyone's life, every day. From something as mundane as facing yet another rainy day, to something as significant as losing the job promotion you thought you had tucked safely in your back pocket, to hiring that blue chip prospect who ended up not showing up for work, the gravity of life maintains that pull and continuously brings you back to Earth. Things happen. They happen to us all. It is what you do about it in the face of challenge that makes the difference between success and failure.

Have you ever gone out to your car and found the tire was flat? How did you feel? What did you think? Were you in a hurry to get somewhere? The gravity of life is like a slap in the face. One minute all is well and before you can pass "go" and collect your two hundred dollars, the garage door no longer opens at the push of a button, your furnace conks out in the midst of a cold spell, the washing machine ceases to spin, and your car dies ... all in the same month. That is the gravity of life. Such misfortune may derail you, but the question is how long do you allow it to keep you mired in your misery? Do you jump up and solve the problem or do you keep that problem circuitously running through your mind without solving the problem and moving forward?

The most successful people deal with the problem directly and do not blame others or feel sorry for themselves. They do not say, "Oh, this always happens to me. Nothing ever goes right for me. Why does this always happen to me?"

When you engage in negative self-talk, your mind tries to answer the questions rather than work to solve the actual problem. Saying "Why does this always happen to me?" is a monomaniacal statement that focuses all the energy on you, the person, and not the problem. Successful people take what happens at face value and treat it like a problem to be solved. They treat it as an obstacle to jump over, not a brick wall to run into. Their self-talk is different. Their self-talk goes something like this: "What do I need to do to solve this problem? Who can help me solve this issue? Where do I need to go to solve this problem?" Notice the difference in invoking self-talk and languishing as a victim to employing self-talk that empowers your mental capabilities? Successful people see what they can do rather than dwell on what happened. The gravity of life is always going to pull you down, but the more important thing to remember is how you deal with that pull. This will all depend on how you look at the situation.

CHAPTER 3

It is Just Not Worth Focusing on the Two Percent!

One of my most memorable trips occurred when my brother Mark invited the entire family to his destination wedding in a city of the Dominican Republic called La Romana, about an hour south of Punta Cana. The trip started early on a Monday. We arose for our flight at around 4:00 a.m. As I completed preparations, I took a final check of my luggage. I realized I needed to throw one or two more things into my bag. Since I had not traveled internationally in about four years, I wanted to make sure I had everything I would need for the trip. We got to the airport at around 6:00 a.m. to catch our 8:20 a.m. flight to Punta Cana. Since I had not been on an airplane in four years, I was particularly excited to fly again.

Sixty family members and friends were boarding the plane on this early October Monday morning for a seven-day, all-inclusive trip to a top-notch four-star resort. I have been to the Dominican Republic before, so I was excited to get there, since I knew what awaited all of us. Everything was to be included in our trip: food, drinks, poolside bars, swim-up bars, splendid service, marvelous entertainment, and a gym staffed with a personal trainer.

Next to the gym was a wonderful relaxing spa, tennis courts, a plethora of beach activities, and 24-hour room service, where I would find myself ordering indescribably scrumptious and satisfying cheeseburgers, whether I was hungry or not. All of the services and activities were at our fingertips, not to mention the option of partaking in the paid excursions the resort offered.

After checking our bags, we finally boarded the airplane and embarked on our three-and-a-half-hour flight. We landed in Punta Cana and boarded a bus that took us directly to the resort. When we arrived at the resort, I was not disappointed. It was magnificent. I came to discover that the number of amenities exceeded my expectations and knowledge of what they had to offer.

As the week wore on, however, I started to hear people grumbling about the very things I believed to be great assets of the resort. I wondered what people could possibly find to complain about, given what the resort, staff, and programming had to offer. I listened as one member of our group criticized how his cheeseburger was cooked. He had made a very specific and unusual request that would have been difficult for even an English-speaking server to understand. When the food arrived and he realized it was not prepared to his specifications, he became visibly upset with the waitstaff. This was the same cheeseburger my taste buds demanded I order. What was puzzling to me was hearing him order the burger every day, and then carp every time it arrived when it was not cooked to his expectations. I also heard others grumble about the food, the spa, waitstaff, the time it took to get their food, the seaweed in the ocean—you name it, they found some fault with it. With all of this luxury at our beck and call, I became perplexed at these pervasively negative perspectives. I could not help but wonder, "Why are they complaining and why are they so upset with things?"

Personally, I felt thankful that I was a part of this trip and wonderful event. As my brother and I debriefed one day following yet another supper of discontent, Mark helped me recognize the basis of the complaining. He said, "No matter what people have, they always find something to complain about. With this guy, you have all this, and he focuses on the two percent that is wrong and not the ninety-eight percent that is right."

I thought about that for just a second and realized it was not the problem itself that was the issue, but the perspective of the person. Perhaps it was not obvious to me right away, since I was accustomed to searching for a deeper explanation of the thoughts and feelings of a person's experience. In reality, it was the age-old question we ask when pouring water into a cup: Is the cup half empty or is the cup half full?

The answer to this question depends on how you view life. If you see that glass as half empty, you probably look at your world with a deficient mentality. If you see it as half full, you generally look at your world with an abundant mentality. Do you see the world with deficiencies or abundance? Do you look for what is wrong or what is possible? These are good questions to ask yourself when looking at a situation or even determining why you feel the way you do. If you are trying to solve a problem, look at the possible solutions (glass half full). If you are analyzing something, it may make sense to search for what is wrong (half empty) so that you can ultimately make it right. You must be prepared to look at both deficiencies and abundance. In our daily lives, viewing the world as half full and focusing on the ninety-eight percent that is right rather than the two percent that is wrong manifests happiness. However, what happens when you are faced with a situation where ninety-eight percent is wrong and two percent is right? With some practice, this too becomes second nature when you allow yourself to keep your eye on the prize and maintain your focus on that measly two percent that is right. It is not easy when you first try it, but it does get easier with practice.

The media bombards us with the wrong doings of our public officials, celebrities, professional athletes, law enforcement, educators, and the common folk. Turn on the television, pull up any search engine home page, read the newspaper, or listen to the radio. They all illustrate why so many people look at the world as half empty. No wonder most people feel so negative.

Unfortunately, this type of news seems to draw people's attention. So, if you are bombarded daily, how can that not have some impact on your outlook? I am not saying that being exposed to all of this media results in a half-empty attitude. I am merely saying that we have to choose the level and context of the exposure so that negativity does not override a sense of accomplishment and happiness. If you are exposed only to the negative realm of life, this is what you are most likely to share with your colleagues, your spouse, and your friends as you review the war in the Middle East, the neighborhood shootings, and the tornado in Kansas that destroyed forty houses. The proverbial straw that may break the camel's back is watching your beloved local football team face a heartbreaking loss. Now everyone is depressed, at least through Monday. Get the point!

Is Your Cup Half Empty or Half Full?

I believe that misfortune and havoc have existed for years. However, we are now in an age where communication is so ubiquitous and available that it intrudes into our lives on a twenty-four/seven basis. Because of that, I believe that half-empty thinking is *part exposure, part training, and part habit*.

Exposure to information is at an unprecedented level. Television, radio, computers, phones, newspapers, tabloids, and social media constantly bombard you with information. What are you checking when you reach for your phone? The latest Facebook post? The latest tweet? How does it all affect you?

You can also be trained by others to communicate in a *half-empty* manner. Consider the people you talk to on a daily basis. Do most of your colleagues complain, or do they look at the bright side of things? These associations color your world and meld into behavior patterns, and you will find yourself looking at life as either half empty or half full. The mere association with complaining or acclaiming is a habit that can and will be established only by you.

People who look at the world as half empty give off negative energy. This negativity becomes contagious. You have encountered this type of person, right? You are at a cocktail party, there is a good verve in the room, the conversation is flowing, and people are having a good time, and then *bam*, Debbie from the fiscal department offers a showstopper of a statement! A hush falls over the room and you and those around you turn your heads and stare, as if to say, "Where the ... did *that* come from?" She is the one who can bring everyone down and suck the oxygen out of the room, dousing it in an awkward silence. It does not take much to look at things in a half-empty way, but it does take energy to reframe it in the positive, look at things from a different perspective, and see the advantages to a situation instead of dwelling on what is always wrong.

If you find yourself mired in a half-empty world, you need to break the habit and start thinking about "positive possibilities." It will make you feel better in the end. If something comes up that is of a negative nature, you can quickly turn it around and give the half-full perspective. Keep doing this and you will cause others to do the same. If you find someone going half empty on you, just ask, "What is the upside to that outlook, and how is it advantageous?" Just one question may increase awareness and turn someone from half empty to half full.

CHAPTER 4

Five Obstacles You Will Need to Jump Over to Get What You Want in Life

My great concern is not whether you have failed, but whether you are content with your failure.
—Abraham Lincoln

Obstacle #1

Fear: Being Afraid Does Not Mean You are Fearful

Fear is the pervasive emotion that can hold people back from realizing potential when facing challenges. Fear may fall into one of these categories, or even some combination thereof: fear of the failure, fear of the unknown, fear of success.

What are you really afraid of? To answer this question, consider ancient times, when man became the advanced hominid species we now know so well. Since fear is at the most primal level of our being, we should start with man's most basic survival needs.

When ancient man failed at the hunt, he went home empty-handed and hungry. That hunger turned into starvation, and he and his family eventually starved to death. When he failed to make a fire, he got cold and eventually froze to death. When he failed to protect his family from other tribes, he was killed. Our fear is primordial and is based on the most basic need to survive.

The fear of dying keeps us alive. Our biology is programmed to keep us alive. Even in our modern day, we still have these fears and they remain programmed in our genes. Modern day society has changed, but our biology has not. Let me prove it.

One of the most common fears is a fear of public speaking. Why are most people afraid of talking in front of others? The fear of public speaking ranks higher than dying. Why? Humans are social animals. We depend on each other for our survival as a species. Acceptance into a group is of great importance to our survival. A person alone can survive for only so long. A society of people can survive for generations. Being part of a family, a group, an organization, a business, and a society is the key to man's survival. So, why would you rather die than give a speech? The underlying primordial fear is that your communication will not be accepted. At the deepest level within ourselves, if the message we portray is not accepted, (our subconscious believes) it could result in us being shunned and ultimately vanquished from the group. Once eliminated from the group, you will no longer receive your share of food from the group hunt, you will get hungry, you will not be permitted to mate to pass on your genes, and you will die lonely and hungry. This is all because you spoke to the group! It makes sense why people are scared to death to talk in front of others. Who wants to die lonely and hungry? I sure do not. Fear is in all of us, and it starts with the desire to survive.

Why are kids (and some adults) afraid of the dark? When you are engulfed in darkness, "unknowns surround you" and you start to believe that not only can the dark be scary, but it can also be deadly. The problem occurs when you generalize this fear to a future replete with "unknowns." If you cannot see what is out there and do not know what will happen, then bad things will happen. Your imagination leads you to dwelling on the worst-case scenario that could occur if you take that dark, scary path, or tackle that "unknown." You do not always know what you are afraid of, and even when you can identify your specific fears, you may struggle to come to terms with it. The fear takes over, stops you from trying, and nothing new is learned.

Millions of years ago, when man first inhabited Earth, he had one thing in common with all other animals. Whether he was the hunter or the hunted, this one common genetic feature was essential to his survival. The common factor was fear. Above all else, the instinctive fear of harm (death) is the most commonly shared attribute among mammals, birds, fish, and reptiles. In all animals, when danger is perceived, real or imagined, the adrenal gland triggers a cocktail of hormonal responses and causes many physiological and psychological responses that prepare the body for "fight or flight," and can be what makes all the difference in survival. When you perceive danger, your heart beats faster in order to circulate blood quicker, thereby providing more oxygen to the muscles for both strength and endurance. The increased blood flow also allows your brain to process information faster. Further, the adrenal gland releases a huge amount of adrenaline to increase awareness and agility.

Without a doubt, these instinctual survival mechanisms are why you and I are here today, and to that extent, they have proven to be extraordinarily effective. These tools have given us the ability to discuss this topic while inside a warm building, even if it is bitter cold outside. It is why we are able to shop at a grocery store and buy a frozen pizza to cook in our oven. It is why we have all the conveniences of modern life, such as microwave ovens, automobiles, washing machines, the internet, safe drinking water, and so on.

The problem is that our technological society and all of its benefits have evolved faster than the biology of man. In many ways, man's evolution is incongruent with technology. This is why the ability to adapt becomes so crucial. Biological evolution is painfully slow, but technological evolution is exponentially fast. Think about it. Five hundred years ago, most people thought the earth was flat. Now scientists are pondering if our universe is only a small part of "The Multiverse." One hundred years ago, man was only first learning to fly; now moon landings are passé and we have set our sights on Mars. Twenty years ago, hardly anyone had a cell phone; now, nearly all of us not only have a cell phone, but our smartphones also allow us to carry the internet in our pocket. While all of this has been going on, the biology of man has remained unchanged. Do you think your biological composition is much different from Christopher Columbus, Orville and Wilbur Wright, or even Steve Jobs?

The point is that our biological responses have

remained unchanged for thousands of years, but our environment has changed so incredibly much. In many ways, our biological mechanisms are outdated, even counterproductive. We are actually inhibiting ourselves.

I am sure this has happened to most of us. You are driving to work and someone cuts you off in traffic. Assuming you do not want to go to jail, all you really can do is slam on the brakes and honk your horn. Very quickly, the danger is gone, yet for the rest of the day, you feel agitated and may even act out inappropriately. You might be short-tempered with the guy taking your order at McDonald's. Your coworkers may find themselves the target of your misplaced annoyance. On your way home from work, you may subconsciously become an aggressive driver yourself. Twelve hours later, you are still feeling agitated. Why? Why are you still angry? After all, the threat of danger was hours ago.

The reason is because the adrenal gland acted the same way it did ten thousand years ago, when a lion was about to capture your ancestors for his dinner. Today, you controlled your physical response because you did not want to go to jail. Your muscles were unable to expend the tremendous amount of adrenaline that you produced. So, quite literally, you have this built-up energy ready to explode. So, what do you do? You direct that energy, albeit misguided, onto others. Remember, this is "fight or flight" energy, not compassionate and loving energy. If a lion were chasing you, you would not be thinking about happy rainbows and pretty flowers, but rather how to evade or kill the lion.

Can you identify with this story? On a cognitive level, you may have been thinking to yourself, "Yeah, everyone gets cut off in traffic. But I never respond like that." However, I will bet that on an emotional level, you were right there with me. If you were indeed able to relate it to a similar situation you experienced, we need to take inventory: Did your heartbeat become elevated? Did you clench your fists? Did you grit your teeth? Did you feel anxious because you were recalling the feeling of helplessness to do anything? Could you imagine yourself screaming at the guy that cut you off, even though you are fully aware that he cannot hear you? Think about it. Why would any of these responses happen? They do not serve any purpose if someone cuts you off in traffic. Probably the worst that would happen would be a fender-bender. After all, you do not have any lions chasing you in this scenario.

Man's instinctive response to fear has been greatly beneficial, but in the twenty-first century, it can be counterproductive. Let me explain: Lions, tigers, and bears are no longer hunting us. However, our subconscious brain is not aware of that. We still have a primordial reaction to fear. How we combat that fear is a key component to achieving success.

Out of all the fears people have that stop them from trying new and exciting ventures, the biggest one is the fear of failure. Fear of failure means a loss and the resulting negative impact on self-esteem, self-efficacy, self-worth, and acceptance from others. These all work against the psyche, handcuffing you to take chances and stretching to different levels. Trying something and not succeeding (or not trying at all) can affect your ability to step out of your comfort zone and produce the results for which you are striving.

Obstacle #2

You Have a Serious Dilemma: Good Things Turning Bad

In Africa, when hunters want to catch a monkey, they use a strategy that exploits the monkey's behavior patterns—patterns that in this case work against the monkey's best interests. The hunter takes a jar with an opening slightly larger than a monkey's hand. The hunter ties a rope around the neck of the jar using a knot, called a monkey's knot, which is a cradle of rope around the jar that secures it tightly to the tree. The hunters then fill the jar with morsels like rice or a banana slice, the favorite food of the monkey. This clever trap works by use of a classic vase-like shape: wide at the top, narrow toward the middle, and open wide at the bottom.

So, how does this trap work? Well, when the unsuspecting monkey notices the jar containing his favorite food, he reaches his hand into the jar and grabs the food, which he clenches in his fist. He starts to pull his arm out, but his clenched fist is unable to move through the narrowest part of the jar. Frantically, with food in hand, the starving primate thrashes about desperately as he struggles, pulls, jumps, and twists, to no avail. He is unable to release himself from the jar as he holds tightly to his food. Now, this is where the monkey has a dilemma. He cannot get his hand out of the jar unless he drops the food. The neck of the jar is simply not wide enough. Of course, the monkey could drop the food and easily get his hand out, but he does not. Despite having a means of escape at his command, he does not. The animal continues to grasp tightly to the food until the hunter throws a net over it, capturing it.

You ask, "Why doesn't the monkey simply open his little monkey paw, release the food, pull his arm from the jar, and escape the hunters?" That would be logical, and for self-preservation sake, that is the obvious solution. So why does he remain trapped? Is it the ultimate desire for the food? Not really. It is the monkey's focus on the food that traps him. He was not able to change his focus from food to danger, and that was ultimately his demise.

Is this relevant to you? You bet it is. You have held on to past thoughts, worries, ideas, and experiences for too long. What was the consequence? You probably experienced lost sleep, failed concentration, an acute sense of unease, or even depression. The parade of life presents you with a variety of experiences, both good and bad, but the inability to let go, especially to the negative ones, plays a part in determining the future quality of life.

Consider how you may have held onto failed relationships, a negative remark you heard about you, the sale that slipped through your fingers, or the promotion that you did not get. These are just a few examples of some common life occurrences that you may psychologically hold in your head. As a result, they stymie your ability to move forward in life. Like the monkey not letting go, these are the obsessive thoughts that throb in your head, nagging you at all hours of the night or day.

When you refuse to let go, you allow the scars of past events to slowly crush your future dreams. One of the main barriers to success and happiness is the inability to let go of the pervasive thoughts, thus negating the option of adopting more empowering ones. So many people allow themselves to remain mired in this negativity and cannot, or will not, move forward.

Go back to the monkey. What really trapped the monkey? Was it the monkey's inability to let go of the food so he could achieve freedom? Holding on to something that was ostensibly good for him ultimately was the animal's demise. It was the belief he needed to keep holding and pulling, even though he was producing no result. Have you done that at times? How can you move forward if you are still holding on to the past?

By holding onto the things that trap you mentally and physically, you are likely to discover the negative consequences associated with this behavior. Christina Enevoldsen reflected on this by saying, "The inability to get something out of your head is a signal that shouts, 'Don't forget to deal with this!' As long as you experience fear or pain with a memory or flashback, there is a lie attached that you need to confront. In each healing step, there is a truth to be gathered and a lie to discard."

Not discarding the lie arrests your movement forward and halts your ability to be successful and happy at a level you deserve. Holding on to untruths, negative feelings, or past problems does not result in solutions. You need to change your thoughts, change your feelings, and ultimately change your behavior.

Have you ever jumped up, grabbed onto the bar, holding your total body weight, and held on until you could not hold on any longer? What happens? First, your hands start to sweat, which makes it harder to hold on. Since your hands start to slip away from the bar, you squeeze the bar even more. This makes the muscles in your hands and forearms cramp up, making it more difficult to hold on. Finally, the combination of your hands perspiring, muscles cramping, and your hands noticeably slipping away provide you with a choice: you can either let go and jump down on your own or you can let your hands slip, resulting in a fall off the bar. This is what you face when you give yourself the one option of desperately holding on to something because it is comfortable and safe. Grabbing the bar is safe, at first. You can hold on just fine for the moment, but you can do so for only a limited amount of time. No matter how strong you are, your strength will eventually run out and you will fall. While holding on feels safe in the short term, eventually you will become so uncomfortable that you will unceremoniously fall.

Obstacle #3

Ask Yourself, Why am I Doing This?

One of my favorite little anecdotes involves the "End of the Ham," which illustrates the notion of doing things without asking why.

The story goes like this:

A man comes home from work and asks, "What's for dinner, sweetheart?"

She matter-of-factly responds, "Ham. But could you please go to the store and pick it up?"

He says, "Of course. I'll be back soon."

So, the man goes to the store and picks up the ham. When he returns home with it, his wife says, "Honey, you didn't have the butcher cut the end of it off."

He responds, "No, you didn't tell me to have the end of it cut off."

Sighing, she retorts, "I always have the end cut off."

Puzzled, he asks, "Why do you have the end of the ham cut off?"

She says, "Because my mother always cut the end off before cooking it."

Becoming quite curious, the man makes a phone call to his mother-in-law and asks, "Why do you cut the end of the ham off before cooking it?"

The mother-in-law responds, "Because my mother always cut the end of it off before cooking it."

The husband, now on a mission to discover the mystery of the truncated meat, calls Grandma and asks, "Grandma, why do you cut the end of the ham off before you cook it?"

Grandma answers, "I cut the end of the ham off so it will fit in my small roaster."

In similar fashion, a newly married couple was cooking together and the wife asked her husband to pass the canned goods to her. When she took the can, she turned it upside down and opened it from the bottom. The husband asked her why she did this and she said, "I really don't know. My mother always opened cans that way. He later asked his mother-in-law why she did that and she said, "When I brought the cans up from the basement, the tops were always dusty. I didn't want to take the time to clean the tops off, so I turned them upside down to open them."

The moral of the stories: Originally, there was a logical reason for cutting off the end of the ham and opening the can from the bottom. Oftentimes we do not have reasons why we do something; we just move from task to task, not questioning the reasons why we do something. We learn from others, but neglect to ask why. This begins in childhood. "Just do what I say and don't ask why," and when we asked why, we were told, "Because I said so." So the conditioning is either a natural response to our parents, or it was more harshly conditioned into our psyche that we are to do what we are told without question.

The next time you are immersed in your morning routine or in a mundane household task such as washing dishes, folding laundry, or putting your silverware away, ask yourself: Is there a reason for folding the shirt this way? Do I need to wash the dishes this way and not another way?

Once you can get into the habit of asking questions, your awareness increases and your personal power is restored. Your power to make informed decisions increases and your ability to create change is much easier and simpler. Being stuck in a rut does not happen overnight; it only happens after weeks, months, and years of hanging onto the same old beliefs and behaviors. The problem occurs when there is a change in your environment and you find you are unable to adapt because of routines that you never bothered to question.

The inability to recognize patterns of behavior and to subsequently change those behaviors that are detrimental or ineffective is even more dangerous for people in business. Consider a company introducing a new computer system to staff, only to have John, the VP of the marketing department, who is sitting in the back of the room, bark out, "Why are we changing it now? The old one works just fine." The manager at the front of the room acknowledges, "I'm not sure why we're changing things, but that is the way it is going to be. So, we're going to have to live with it." There are two problems with this scenario. First, John appears resistant to this change in computer systems and, perhaps, rightfully so. He has a valid question. However, the real problem is that the manager did not have a good reason as to why the company is changing systems. It is imprudent for companies to expect employees to abandon a tried and trusted tool or technique that has allowed them to perform their jobs successfully without giving them a valid reason for doing so.

In the article "All in the Family" by Brooke Bates, the author tells the story of one of Pittsburgh, Pennsylvania's most iconic and successful specialty food stores, McGinnis Sisters Special Food Stores. The book describes the evolution of their business and how they made the changes necessary to stay competitive. The company is in their third generation of owners. Elwood McGinnis grew the business from a small produce stand in 1946 to a supermarket. During this transformation, all eight McGinnis children grew up in the shadow of the family business, some even in playpens behind the checkout counter. Elwood McGinnis retired in 1981. Sisters Bonnie McGinnis Vello, Noreen McGinnis Campbell, and Sharon

McGinnis Young took over the growing company, which became the Pittsburgh-based McGinnis Sisters Special Food Stores.

Like any company that grows and attains success, the sustainability of that company results from knowing the ever-changing wants and needs of the consumer. Noreen McGinnis Campbell had an uncanny ability for doing exactly that. However, when confronting market adjustments and the ever-changing needs of the customer, tradition and familiarity can create unforeseen obstacles. This was what faced Noreen McGinnis Campbell, vice president and owner. She is quoted in the article as saying, "We were very young when we took over … it was kind of a rocky transition, but my dad was still around in the wings of the business to help. What I think he struggled with was the change in product mix, why we weren't doing things the old ways, as he had done. I remember saying, 'Dad, we have to do it differently.'"

Even though there were changes in products, the core values were kept close to their hearts and continued to guide the company in choosing the best foods, treating employees like family, treating customers like friends, and giving back to the community. Not only were they able to make changes in products that were necessary to meet consumer demands, but they were also able to maintain a grasp on the core values. In order to remain on the cutting edge of the business, the decision was made that the next generation of owners needed to work elsewhere for a time to gain the experience and perspective needed when it was eventually time to return to work for McGinnis Sisters.

That is exactly what happened. The employees were able to acquire new skills and gain perspectives that they were able to integrate into future business decisions in an increasingly complex work environment. Like all great business owners, they realized that the business must continue to evolve. Jennifer Daurora, Bonnie's daughter, is in charge of business development and is quoted in the article as saying, "(In the future) when our transition may be complete in the legal sense, it will never really be complete. We're always evolving, and I want to be able to come to my family members, ask their thoughts and opinions, and gain their wisdom."

Obstacle #4

I'm Helpless: Who Do I Blame Now?

Dog Experiment

The theory of learned helplessness was conceived in 1967 by U.S. psychologists Martin Seligman and Steve Maier at the University of Pennsylvania as an extension of their interest in depression. Seligman and his colleagues conducted learned helplessness experiments in which they exposed dogs to aversive stimulus that they could not escape. Eventually, the animal stops trying to avoid the stimulus and behaves as if it is helpless to change the situation. When opportunities to escape become available, learned helplessness means that the animal does not take any action.

This is illustrated in the most famous experiment that Seligman and Maier performed. They tested three groups of dogs in a shuttle-box apparatus, where dogs could escape electric shocks by jumping over a low partition.

From a previous experiment, in which the dogs were exposed to electric shocks with no means of escape, they learned that nothing they did had any effect on avoiding the shocks. Therefore, they simply lay down passively and whined. Even though the dogs could have easily escaped the shocks in the new experiment, they did not try. The psychologists deemed the lack of attempt as a retardation of learning. They concluded that the dogs' initial response to the shock was so overwhelming that it made it difficult to change that response even when escape was possible. As a result, the dogs learned to be helpless, and exhibited symptoms similar to chronic clinical depression.

Baby Experiment

Other experiments performed on different animals had similar results. In all cases, the strongest predictor of a depressive response was lack of control over the aversive stimulus. One such experiment, presented by Watson & Ramey (1969), consisted of two groups of human babies. They placed one group of babies into a crib with a sensory pillow, designed so that the movement of the baby's head could control the rotation of a mobile. The other group had no control over the movement of the mobile and could only enjoy looking at it. Later, they tested both groups of babies in cribs equipped with the pillows that allowed the babies to control the mobile. Although all the babies now had the power to control the mobile, only the group that had already learned about the sensory pillow attempted to use it.

Mental Tasks

Another example of this phenomenon involved an experiment in which people had to perform mental tasks in the presence of distracting noise. People who could use a switch to turn off the noise performed significantly better, even though they rarely bothered to do so. Simply being aware of this option was enough to substantially counteract the distracting effect.

In 2011, an animal study found that animals with control over stress exhibited changes in the excitability of specific neurons within the prefrontal cortex, and modeled this phenomenon in a conductance-based neural simulation. Animals that lacked control failed to exhibit an increase in excitability and showed signs consistent with learned helplessness and social anxiety.

Let me share my own experience with learned helplessness. My son came to me one Saturday morning with one of his toys and said, "Daddy, can you fix this?" It was one of those remote control cars that had been zipping around our house incessantly for the past few days. Usually, I assess the problem, make a few adjustments (most times easy fixes), give the toy back to him, and send him on his way. This time was different. I looked at the car, unscrewed the bottom, changed the batteries—encompassing the extent of my mechanical prowess—turned it on, and ... nothing. I grabbed my handy screwdriver, took most of the car apart, jiggled a few wires, put it back together, and it still did not work. After working on it for quite a long time, I simply gave up and had to break it to my son that I could not correct the problem and that the car would never run again. We would need to buy another one.

Have you ever tried to repair a toy or work on a task that you could not fix, solve, or correct, even after hours or days? Finally, you simply give up. I think we all have had these experiences at one time or another. Calling it quits from time to time is not unusual; it is quite normal and probably healthy at some level. Allowing yourself to move on from a failed task can give you the flexibility and faith you'll need the next time you are confronted with a challenge. It is only when you feel that there are no options that you can feel helpless. When you do not think, feel, or believe you have options in life, you can acquire this condition of *Learned Helplessness* or *Conditioned Defeat*.

Learned helplessness also happens in organizations where you find supervisors towering over their employees and flexing their managerial muscles by micromanaging every aspect of their employees' jobs, only to destroy their sense of personal power, autonomy, and professional leadership. Over time, the fire employees once had for their work is snuffed out like a candle flame. There is an almost palpable feeling of the oxygen being sapped from the room, the last breath being the resignation of the employees. It is as if the staff had been placed in a box like the dogs in the shuttle box and shocked daily by having their work shot down over and over again.

Supervisors must recognize that a sense of accomplishment is one of the most important factors in a person's work. If a boss continually criticizes an employee's work with no regards to the process, the employee experiences an emotional shock. Eventually, the cumulative result of the shocks handcuffs the employee's confidence, their self-esteem ebbs, and eventually performance grinds to a halt.

Organizations find themselves in a quandary as to why retaining staff is so difficult. People learn to be helpless in these circumstances. When an employee's personal power is zapped away, ensuing collateral damage occurs in an agency's reputation and profit. The employee starts to give up, performance declines, productivity falls, and a negative attitude creeps in, spawning a toxic environment that customers start to feel and experience. The satisfaction that is generated from how employees feel about their work affects the customer's experience and ultimately relates to the retention of business. If employees feel empowered by their work, they will embrace the company's mission, take pride in their work, and genuinely care about how the customer receives and perceives the delivery of services.

Creating such a culture starts at the top, where the executive team, directors, and supervisors must provide the space, creativity, and ingenuity to produce a sense of meaning for the work by emphasizing collaboration rather than disunion. Further, employees' satisfaction with the work environment is directly proportional to how they perform their job and subsequently treat the customer. Of course, the natural consequence is customer retention and loyalty that becomes the keystone of doing business.

Obstacle #5

Walking the Tightrope of Life and Keeping Your Balance

One of my first courses in college was a physiology class. The first subject matter we covered in this course was the biological process of homeostasis. Homeostasis keeps the body in balance by having all corresponding functions working in stable harmony to keep your body working perfectly. When you get cold, your body starts to shiver to heat the body in order to drive your internal temperature to where it should be so you do not freeze. When you get too hot, you perspire to cool down so your body does not overheat. Your body is always working to adjust to the environment to maintain life.

Astronomers tell us that Earth maintains an orbit around our star in just the right position to sustain life. If the earth was any closer to the sun, the earth's oceans would evaporate, and our planet would become barren and dry, just like its neighbors, Mercury and Venus. If Earth was any further away from the sun, our planet would be a mass of frozen rock and ice. Being positioned in just the right place is what astronomers call the circumstellar habitable zone (CHZ). Colloquially, this is known as the Goldilocks zone … "it's just right." Specifically, this is the region around a star where planetary-mass objects with sufficient atmospheric pressure can support liquid water at their surfaces.

Children manage to keep things balanced. It might not look like it, but they do. This happens all the time in my house. My kids will be playing in bliss all by themselves, with not a worry in the world, so my wife and I will start talking. As soon as this happens, invariably, one of our children must insert themselves into the conversation. If you are a parent, I am sure this has happened to you. What is happening here? What does this have to do with homeostasis? If you know anything about children, their number one need is attention. If they are not getting it, they are quite clever about finding ways to do so, either by being rude or engaging in any type of behavior that necessitates a response. If the child does not get the needed attention, he turns the behavior up a notch. In essence, the child "heats things up" to get the needed attention in one manner or another, because to a child, homeostasis is achieved when their needs are being met.

Considering a broader scope, the same thing happens within the family unit. Our own families need to maintain a homeostatic environment to keep things in balance. Family dynamics and interactions make this happen. Members of the family behave in different ways to keep that balance. One parent may be rigid, the other lenient, while one child is outgoing and verbal and the other is introspective.

Societies seek to maintain homeostasis as well. For example, stock markets adjust and self-correct to keep the money flowing. We shy away from politicians who are too far left or right, seeking someone "in the middle of the road."

It all starts with you. You are a thermostat. If you get too cold, you crank up the heat. When you get too warm, you turn it down. You may not even realize you are doing this (or maybe you do), but you are continually making adjustments to your environment. Why? Homeostasis. Keeping things balanced is a survival tactic streaming from physiology into society. Though you are physiologically programmed to do this, sometimes it is not advantageous. You need to experience discomfort for a while and allow yourself time to adjust to it. If you always seek comfort and keep changing the environment to achieve it, you will not experience growth. Part of growing is adapting to uncomfortable situations and creating a "new norm." Self-sabotage is a behavior that can happen when you are confronted with a situation that is out of your comfort zone!

Once you recognize and deal with the limiting factors hindering your behavior and preventing you from reaching the levels of success you want to achieve, you can then learn, develop, and explore strategies that allow you to reach whatever you desire and deserve in your life. This next section will build that foundation for you.

PART 2

The Building Blocks to Your Success

CHAPTER 5

Play to Win

The problem is that most people do not realize they can affect change, and thus are content to maintain their current status, which translates to playing not to lose. However, playing to win is a far superior and productive mindset. In sports, playing not to lose or holding onto a lead gives the other team time to catch up and win the game. When you play "not to lose," it is merely giving others an opportunity and depriving yourself of one that may ultimately contribute to your failure. While you are taking the safe route and playing not to lose, there are others scheming to make you lose. As a result, you are stacking the odds against yourself.

Consider this: The hockey team is up three goals to two, with five minutes to go in the game, and all of a sudden, it happens. The aggressive offensive play that contributed to early success now becomes a game of defense. You notice nervousness draping over the team. Holding on desperately to the lead, they start to block every shot, not even attempting to take the puck up the ice to the opponent's goal. As probability dictates, when the opposing team takes shot after shot, the puck eventually sneaks past the defender and the goalie. He shoots and scores! Now the score is tied and all the momentum is in favor of the other team. If you are a hockey fan, you have seen this more than once. Within minutes of tying the game, the puck is dropped at the faceoff, and with two sharp passes up the ice, he shoots, he scores, and arms fly up, indicating they just came back and won. Playing not to lose is not the way to go, particularly in this case.

The same is true in business. If a company is not looking to move forward, they are giving their competitors the opportunity to "play to win." Companies that conduct business this way will, over the course of six months or six decades, usually find themselves struggling to maintain their existence. Remember, if you are not climbing, you are falling. A perfect example of this is Facebook. Over the past few years, Facebook has bought out any start-up site that may be a problem for them down the road. They have spent tens of billions of dollars to do so. This is playing to win.

Consider the railroad and oil tycoons from much earlier in this country's history. They undercut their competitors by selling their goods and services at a rate far below cost. This was a calculated risk to make their competitors unable to sustain such a competition for long, and they quickly looked to sell out to the larger company. This is playing to win.

Another example is President Kennedy's bold challenge and proclamation to land on the moon before the end of the decade in spite of the countless questions and inherent risks. This is playing to win and worthy of a more extensive analysis.

First, President Kennedy's challenge can more accurately be described as a commitment. Not just any commitment, but a commitment to win. At the time of his challenge, the United States was losing the "Space Race" to the Soviet Union. The Soviet Union had been first in accomplishing every major milestone in space, which was part of the larger arms race. It was becoming clear that the developing technology of rockets and satellites and their capabilities was going to define the future of the two nations. Many believed that falling behind in the arms race was a cataclysmic threat to our survival as a nation; therefore, failure was not an option. What easier commitment could you make than to guarantee your own survival!

Of course, this commitment meant sacrifice. President Kennedy in effect said, "We will not merely try to keep pace with the USSR. We will not 'play not to lose,' but rather we are going to take control of this race." Even though the technology to land on the moon had yet to be developed, President Kennedy put our nation on a path to seek answers rather than belaboring the questions. He was seeking to win rather than "playing not to lose." Lives were lost and billions of dollars spent, but the commitment was there. Indeed, two decades later, President Reagan was continuing JFK's commitment to win by proposing the concept of "Star Wars," in which space-based weapons would protect the United States from a nuclear attack. Taking control and landing men on the moon is certainly a major victory, but let us return to Earth and explore how a little business out of Seattle, Washington, determined how they would play to win their own game.

This particular business launched in Seattle, Washington, when the owners of a humble little coffee shop grew it into a billion-dollar business. You might have heard of it. It is in virtually every city in America and in many countries abroad. The company is none other than

Starbucks. No other company in the coffee business can come close to competing with Starbucks in earnings or branding. Founders Jerry Baldwin, Zev Siegl, and Gordon Bowler opened the first Starbucks in Seattle on March 30, 1971. The name came from the book *Moby Dick* and the chief mate, Starbucks.

Their first venture was selling coffee beans, but in 1984, Jerry purchased Peet's Coffee and Tea and started selling specialty coffee. In 1987, the original owners sold the company to Howard Schultz, a former employee who rebranded his company, Il Giornale, into Starbucks. That year, Howard opened stores in Vancouver, Chicago, and other locations in the Northwest and Midwest. In 1996, Starbucks opened in Tokyo, Japan, the first store outside North America. From 2003 to 2006, Starbucks purchased additional companies, including Seattle's Best, Torrefazione Italia Coffee, Diedrich Coffee, and People's Coffee. In May 2009, Starbucks introduced its loyalty program and mobile app, which further established it as the most dominant coffee company ever to exist. The company's revenue shows this clearly. Starbucks' revenue grew from $1.7 billion in 1999 to a staggering $5.3 billion in 2015.

According to investor.starbucks.com, Howard Schultz, Starbucks chairman and CEO, stated, "Starbucks' record Q1 2016 financial and operating results, highlighted by comp sales increases of nine percent in the U.S., eight percent globally, another four percent increase in global traffic—and record performance from our Channel Development segment—underscore the accelerating strength and relevance of the Starbucks brand around the world. Successful retail, CPG, digital, mobile, loyalty, card and investment strategies, are combining to accelerate our revenue growth and drive significant margin expansion and EPS leverage."

Scott Maw, Starbucks CFO, reinforced Schultz's statement by saying, "We've entered fiscal 2016 with another record-breaking quarter and a continuation of the accelerating momentum we saw in our business throughout 2015. The investments we are making in our people and our business are driving record, industry leading operating and financial performance and consistently strong comp growth, and are both paying off today and setting us up for continued strong performance into the future."

All great companies strive for perfection, and Starbucks is no different. Starbucks sets the highest standards for process, procedure, and employee and customer satisfaction. Many companies strive to reach these standards, but Starbucks was able to reach and maintain their high standards of performance. Starbucks plays to win.

Do you play to win or are you playing not to lose? From sports to business, playing to win, giving it your all, and having trust in the process is the way to go. Consider these five thoughts when you are playing to win:

Have faith and do not be afraid to take chances. If it feels uncomfortable, you are probably in the right place to take the chance and make the move.

Plan to play. It is all right to take chances, but be smart about it. Most times, you must try things in order to learn, but if you are attacking something too impulsively, it can get you in trouble and you may not be able to recover. So plan ahead and then take that calculated risk, and be smart when you go for it.

Whether or not you find yourself hitting the mark, continue to take those shots. The more shots you take, the more you will score. Do not fall back and become defensive. There is a time and place for defense, but do not play defense to hold a lead.

When you play to win, you are playing with courage. When you are playing not to lose, you are playing in fear. Playing to win is an attitude with action and an action with a courageous attitude.

And last, when you play not to lose, you are playing to get through the day. When you play to win, you are playing for tomorrow's future successes.

So, if playing to win is the key to success, why doesn't everyone do it? There are several reasons we do not take action, and in this next section, you will learn the factors that prevent you from playing to win and how to overcome these obstacles.

CHAPTER 6

Increasing Your Expectations Beyond What You Think is Reasonable

I am not in this world to live up to your expectations and you're not in this world to live up to mine.
—Bruce Lee

When Michael Jordan was asked what the secret to his success was, he said, "I asked more from myself than anyone could ever ask from me." That is the trick. You need to internalize your demands for excellence, rather than waiting for someone else to define success for you. Here is where the real magic happens! Once you've established that standard, you need to raise it a notch and expect even more! What it comes down to is defining your expectations and raising them continually and methodically over time, day in and day out, week in and week out, year in and year out. It becomes a never-ending chronicle of your life.

Think of it this way. You are listening to the radio and a song that you like begins to play. You naturally turn the volume up just a notch. You become immersed in the song and gleefully begin to sing along. Then the next song that airs is one you like even more than the first. You crank up the volume one or two more notches. Finally, your absolute favorite song of all time comes on and you really give the speakers all they can handle. At this point, you are singing and shouting along with the artist and giving the ultimate performance of your singing career! Then someone walks in the room and impatiently inquires, "Are you deaf? Turn that down!" You comply while thinking to yourself, "It really isn't that loud."

What happened in this scenario is that over time, you become acclimated to the incremental increases in volume. If you turned it up all the way on the first song, you would have recognized it was too loud and would have turned it down after the song ended. The same holds true with your expectations of yourself. You need to make your expectations incrementally achievable. Once you have met that initial expectation, you need to crank up the volume and ask yourself, "What's next?" When you finally meet expectations and achieve your goal, there is nothing prohibiting you from going further. Do you want to stop climbing the hill just because you have reached the summit, or would you rather look for a steeper hill to tackle?

Within this context of raising your expectations, let us consider Charles Darwin's *Theory of Evolution*. I am sure you are familiar with it, but it clearly illustrates another way you can create your own success. It maintains that through natural selection, adaptability is essential to a species' survival. Because a species' environment is evolving, the species must evolve along with the environment. Therefore, a species must continuously evolve or face the possibility of extinction. This is demonstrated by a multitude of examples, from an ape's opposable thumbs to a chameleon's camouflage. The organism that most effectively adapts in a particular environment will ultimately survive, while those that are less fit struggle to maintain their existence. This *Theory of Evolution* has since yielded what is commonly referred to as *Social Darwinism,* which in turn gave birth to the term with which we are most familiar: "survival of the fittest."

For you to be at your most fit, you must constantly evolve and improve. You need to seek opportunities to increase your knowledge, skills, education, fitness, and health. "Success is opportunity meeting preparation." Humans have a unique ability compared to other species, and that is the *consciousness of choice*. Making choices is the most powerful attribute we have as a species. A tree cannot uproot itself and move to a better climate or choose what to eat or with whom to associate. However, humans do—*you do*. This makes us very special as a species.

You can see that remaining stagnant is counterproductive. You have the ability to change your thoughts, behaviors, routines, and expectations, and ultimately to move ahead to get what you want. You have the ability to make a decision and *act upon it*. You can decide, "I am going to eat an apple today," *and act upon it*. You can decide, "I am going to take a long walk," *and act upon it*. You can decide, "I am going to associate myself with more positive people," *and act upon it*. Conversely, a tree cannot. A tree can only stand rooted in the ground next to the other trees for the next hundred years or so, whether it likes it or not. Since you are not a tree, you have the ability to uproot yourself, make and act on your decisions, and achieve your aspirations while raising them over time.

It is important to understand that increasing your expectations and continuously challenging yourself to accept nothing but your best can be an easy decision, but the difficulty lies in maintaining constant progress toward that goal when faced with barriers that make it seem insurmountable. Obviously, this process will not be completed overnight, which is exactly why you have made a *commitment* of both time and effort.

Think of a mountain climber preparing for the most difficult climb of her life. She must first strategize ascending and descending the mountain before deciding whether she is actually going to undertake the climb. Even if she changes her mind during the climb, she still faces the challenge of descending the mountain. As soon as that initial decision to embark on the climb occurs, she has made a commitment. She is, by nature, defying the gravity of life, the force that is nipping at her heels in an effort to pull her back down from her perch in the clouds to Earth. If she slips and loses her footing, she falls. Once you commit to something, it is imperative to hold onto that commitment lest you destroy the foundation on which all else will be built.

Commitment is not unlike a light switch. When you flip the switch, the light does not decide it will not turn on. Once the switch is in the "on" position, the electricity shoots at the speed of light in one direction to the bulb, and then the light illuminates the room. That is what your attitude toward commitment needs to be. Flip the switch in your mind and make that commitment.

Committing to change is difficult and painful, which is why many people are reluctant to engage in the process of self-improvement. Self-improvement is very much like strengthening a muscle. To build a muscle, you first have to tear it down. To tear down a muscle you must apply intense pressure, exertion, movement, lifting, and moving heavy objects. Simply put, you must exercise. The muscle needs this exercise, even to the point of exhaustion. The actual muscle fibers need to be damaged in order to rebuild. Once the fibers are broken down, the body goes to work to rebuild them back up to their original strength, right?

Actually, it is the opposite. We know that when a muscle is broken down, the body says, "I was just damaged. This could happen again. Let me prepare myself in case this does happen again. So I need to increase muscle mass so that the next time it will not be so easy to damage the muscle." The result is a stronger, larger, more robust muscle. However, the muscle does not stop there. The next time it experiences stress, it goes through the same process as before, but it starts at a higher point. It builds even more muscle fibers, which yields even stronger and larger muscles. The essence of what the muscle is experiencing and how it responds is adaptation. It is constantly improving for the next time it experiences the stress and pressure.

Similarly, you need to continuously adapt in your everyday life in order to not only survive, but also get stronger. The person who fails to adapt to the pressure of life gets weaker and eventually sees no option other than to give up and concede defeat. Successful people are those who have been wrenched down but used the experience to bounce back even stronger than before. My guess is that since you are reading this book, you are aspiring to be the one who rebuilds themselves to be stronger, more durable, more adaptable, and more determined to be successful.

I mentioned earlier that there is no in-between when it comes to either climbing or sliding down the hill of success. This is why it is important to keep improving your skills, knowledge, and overall being. If you do not, the consequence is that the gravity of life slowly, but consistently, gains the advantage.

We can put this in perspective by considering the previous example of how a muscle grows. All things being equal, Person A chooses to be sedentary while Person B chooses to exercise (improve). While Person B gradually becomes stronger over time, Person A remains at the same baseline level. So, in effect, without doing anything wrong, but also without doing anything, Person A is slowly sliding down the hill of success because Person B has elevated the baseline beyond Person A's level of stagnation.

Person A was not by any means a huge blundering failure. He did not make poor choices, have bad luck, or have any defects. Person A simply did nothing and, consequently, Person B passed him by. I mentioned earlier when Michael Jordan was asked what the secret to his success was that he responded, "I asked more from myself than anyone could ever ask from me." By increasing his expectations of himself while his opponents were not doing the same, he was able to lead his team to six NBA championships. Six championships is not a fluke. Remember, you are not a tree; you have the free will to improve your situation.

An important thing to remember is that once you fall behind the pack, you need to work harder than others just to catch up. Again, the baseline has changed. Once you fall behind, you can postpone any notions about gaining an advantage, because you will need to work twice as hard just to regain even footing.

Once you feel yourself slipping down the hill of success, you must ask yourself, What can I do about this? Therein lies the answer to the question. You simply need to begin by asking questions, and the answers will soon follow. Forget about having the answer to every question. If you have only some of the answers and act upon them, you've started the improvement process. In fact, asking questions and seeking the answers is itself an exercise in self-improvement.

Follow the simple guidelines of asking: Who? What? Where? When? Why? and How? Ask yourself: How can I make this better? What can I do to increase the quality? Who can help me to increase the quantity? What aspects of my situation can be improved? When should I implement this or that? What is my target goal? The real trick, however, is that you need to shed your rose-colored glasses and view everything with stark reality.

If you want the process of asking these questions to be most effective, it must be part of your daily routine. If you always view your current situation as a stepping-stone to the next, and if you are always looking ahead, you will find the answers. The most important question you need to consider is: Why should I stop here? It is a rhetorical question that answers itself, and it is the key to keeping you moving forward.

In finding the answer to any particular question, I think it is also important to create a global picture of your life. While you need to have focus in order to achieve any specific goal, you also need to think globally. As the adage goes, *the whole is greater than the sum of its parts.*

You cannot operate an internal combustion engine for long without cooling it. A coolant system is not effective without propulsion. You need wheels, belts, and pulleys. A battery needs to activate them, sustained by an alternator and so forth, until you have all the individual parts of an automobile. The sum of the parts would just be a big pile of metal and plastic bathed in oil. So you see, when they all work together in synchronicity, they form something greater than the sum of the parts—an automobile.

The same is true for your total being. Charles de Lint observed this by saying, "I do believe in an everyday sort of magic—the inexplicable connectedness we sometimes experience with places, people, works of art, and the like; the eerie appropriateness of moments of synchronicity; the whispered voice, the hidden presence, when we think we are alone."

Consider all major aspects of your life: your health (both physical and mental), your relationships, your finances, and your spirituality. Whatever your goal is, if you neglect any one aspect, the others will suffer as well. True success depends on achieving balance among the many facets of your being. Remember, the whole is greater than the sum of its parts. If you have great health but terrible relationships, you may be in for a long but lonely life. If you are wealthy but have terrible health, you will not be around long enough to spend your money. If you have great relationships but cannot maintain them because of poor mental health, you are not likely to experience the contentment of true companionship.

CHAPTER 7

The Champion's Trio: Scoring a Hat-Trick in Life

Our greatest glory is not in ever falling, but in the rising every time we fall.
—Confucius

In this day and age, with things changing at a pace faster than at any other time in history, it is imperative to recognize and embrace these changes, lest you be left in their wake. In this wildly competitive climate, you cannot stand still. There are volumes of research substantiating that the most successful leaders are always looking forward, often many years into the future. They are anticipating and planning for what will happen next. Staying ahead of the curve in your career, business, and life will determine if you succeed or fail. Creating and implementing a strategy that keeps you moving forward and upward allows you to stay ahead of the curve. Without a solid strategy for success, you will start to slide down the proverbial hill that ends in a pool of failure. There is no in-between. You are either climbing or sliding. It is that simple.

For example, you can fall financially by not investing. If you put your money in a savings account and keep it there, inflation will beat your bank's interest rate. Your store of knowledge may plunge if you fail to learn what is new in the realm of technology, industry, and culture in general, as new paradigms reach your business. Of course, an athlete can flounder by not investing in quality training, learning new techniques, increasing conditioning, or scheduling proper rest and recovery time.

Without active and purposeful resistance on your part, the gravity of life simply takes over. It is constantly tugging at you. If you do not fight it, it can drag you down and pull you away from what you want. However, if you actively resist the gravitational pull of lethargy, and you are determined to succeed, you will find yourself ascending toward the summit.

#1 Criticism: Who Really Cares What Others Say

It is better to light a candle than curse the darkness.
—Eleanor Roosevelt

Do you know one of the major factors hindering a person's success? What is it that makes someone either melt in embarrassment or boil in anger? I am excited to share with you not only the answer to these questions, but also a strategy that, if used properly, will improve your performance in any field of endeavor. I will teach you a mental process that all champions possess. Once you learn this process, you will find yourself learning more, performing at a higher level, and achieving whatever it is you are striving toward. Sport scientists say ninety percent of success is mental and the other ten percent is physical. Returning to my initial question posed in the beginning of this section, what is one of the major factors contributing to success?

Quite simply, it is the ability to accept criticism. No doubt, at one time or another, you have all been criticized, and it is human nature to be taken aback by a critical comment. It is indeed a natural defense mechanism. Since you want others to accept and like you, criticism can feel like a dagger stabbing you in the heart. Your ego may become bruised and you may feel the need to defend yourself. Can you recall a time when you were criticized by your parents, your coach, or your supervisor, and found yourself spurting out quick retorts, excuses, and stories as to why your performance was not up to par? This is the ego defending itself, keeping your self-esteem afloat, your self-worth and pride intact. Ego and pride, the two great parts of your psyche, impair your ability to accept critical statements. The problem is that when your pride gets in the way, your defenses rise and learning stops. When learning stops, you cease to develop the necessary skills for success.

We all have something to learn, but if we are too busy defending ourselves, we will never learn, improve, or advance. That goes for all aspects of our lives, whether in sports, education, or business. Losing these valuable opportunities stunts growth and maturity.

What exactly is criticism? Are there different kinds? In its most positive light, it can be seen as "… advice that is useful and intended to help or improve something, often with an offer of possible solutions."

I will instead break this down. First, it states, "… advice that is useful." This means to me that when someone criticizes you, rather than being cruel, they are, in actuality, giving you advice. This will be an important aspect to remember as we continue to explore this subject.

Second, it says, "... intended to help or improve something ..." Usually, we do not associate criticism with "helping or improving." However, criticism can indeed help if you listen closely to what is being said rather than thinking of ways to defend yourself, shutting down, or dismissing the message.

The definition continues "... often with an offer of possible solutions." When criticized, the last thing you hear is any type of a solution being generated. I can tell you that when a coach starts to point things out that you are doing wrong, he or she is giving solutions, such as, "Come on, get your head up," or simply, "Move! Move!" At first blush, this may sound quite negative, but in reality, the coach is presenting solutions to problems with your performance. Indeed, they can be hard to recognize if exclaimed with vigor. Milan Kundera once said, "Without the meditative background that is criticism, works become isolated gestures and historical accidents, soon forgotten."

As you can see, critics are disguised as helpers and solution makers. My question to you is: What kind of person takes criticism and lets it destroy him, and what person takes criticism and uses it to improve? As I posed earlier, are there different kinds of criticism? I believe there are two very distinct forms: constructive and non-constructive. In truth, though, the primary difference between the two is how you interpret the information that is being imparted. How it is said is not nearly as important as what is being said. Therein lies a key element: criticism is only information.

The two types of criticism may in fact be described as hearing what is being said in two very different ways, by two different personality types. The "loser" is likely to define criticism as non-constructive. These are people whose feelings are easily hurt and who are likely to run away when confronted with negative feedback. Losers interpret criticism as a personal attack. They feel hurt, demoralized, deflated, and defeated, and ultimately shut down and quit. As a result, losers never grow. They never expand and they never reach their full potential. They do not have the courage to hear what they did wrong, always walking away with their head down and their tail between their legs. They never play again. They are "losers."

"Winners," on the other hand, interpret criticism as constructive feedback. They feel appreciated, helped, and validated. Winners and champions relish feedback, soaking up everything that is said, and make lemonade out of lemons. Winners see criticism as paving the way to their success. Winners feel that the information serves them and motivates them to do better the next time. Winners see criticism as helpful and useful and are appreciative of the feedback, feeling "psyched" that the coach is paying attention to how they are performing. This makes them work even harder and longer, thirsty for even more feedback. Winners look at criticism as something they can add to their toolbox for their future success. Winners are successful because they are eager to learn more, expand upon their existing skills, and subsequently improve their performances. The winner is the one who looks at the glass half full, not half empty.

When confronted with criticism, are you a loser or are you a winner? I think it is obvious that we all want to be winners. Let me share with you a three-step process that will assist you in listening to criticism and having it serve you, rather than destroy you.

Step 1: First, recognize and note how you initially feel when that critical statement smacks you in the face. Be aware of the shock of embarrassment and hurt, and do not dismiss it.

Step 2: Embrace the feeling and let it run its course. We all get embarrassed and uneasy when someone verbally attacks us. Remember, it is a natural part of our being. Give yourself some time for the emotion to pass. This will not take long, because once you are in the habit of asking the following questions, you will be able to move quickly to the next step.

Step 3: Ask yourself these questions: How does this critique serve me? What does it mean? What is really being transmitted? Is this statement meant to help me in some way? Is it to motivate me? Once you assimilate a few possible answers to these questions, go to Step 4 and ask yourself: How can I use this information to make me better?

Step 4: Take a few moments, think about the content of the comment, and carefully consider how you can use this information. Letting someone ruffle your feathers is a response to protecting your pride and self-respect. After allowing some time and the sting of that initial emotion to pass, you realize they were right. They made a valid point and you should have been more receptive to their message.

So, to review:

Step 1: Acknowledge the feeling.

Step 2: Let the emotion for the criticism pass.

Step 3: Ask several questions to extract the useful content of what was said.

Step 4: Find ways to use this information to make you better.

These are the key steps that will help you use the information and feedback presented. By objectively accepting, assimilating, processing, and then using the feedback, you will be on your way to a successful career!

#2 Failure is Not an Option

Never walk away from failure. On the contrary, study it carefully and imaginatively for its hidden assets.
—Michael Korda

Someone once told me, "Failure is not as important for losers as it is for winners." A loser does not care that he failed. He expects to fail and is quite comfortable with falling short. The comfort manifests itself as excuses. He pulls out the excuse box and opens it up every time he fails. With plenty of excuses added to the toolbox over the years, a loser always has one at the ready to justify why something or someone was not successful.

I will bet you have met your share of losers over the course of time. These people are quick to shift blame and firmly dump the responsibility for failure onto to the lap of others. It is never the loser's fault. However, by not being at fault, losers seldom learn from their mistakes. They are doomed to endlessly repeat the same mistakes, never improving or advancing in life. That is the problem with making excuses. Losers are unable, or unwilling, to accept ownership of their behaviors and therefore cannot move ahead.

On the other side of the coin, there is the winner. Winners never expect to lose or fail. When a winner does fail, it is an extremely painful and heartbreaking experience.

Anger, angst, and disbelief are the prevailing emotions. Put simply, winners fail. Contrary to losers, winners become angry and immediately place the defeat squarely on their own backs. Intensely searching for the reason for failing, winners take total responsibility and analyze every aspect of the experience, desperately trying to come up with answers. Questions race through the winner's mind: What could I have done differently? What did I say or do to manifest the results? How could I have responded differently? Who could have helped me at that time? Winners pore through question after question, thought after thought, always searching for the answers to those questions to ultimately learn from the experience. It is a champion's mindset to accept total responsibility and think objectively through the experience to learn from it and improve his or herself in the hopes of yielding a different outcome in the future.

Not everyone can be so easily categorized as a failure or a champion, though. Most people genuinely want to succeed and reach their goals, but do not. Why? Because they are simply afraid to fail. They know what they need to do, but still they are reluctant to actually take the leap and go "all in," in the quest for achieving their goals.

Why are so many people afraid to fail?

It all starts as young children in school and, for many, even earlier, but I will instead start with school. What does earning a letter grade really mean to a child? What are grades? Are they a reflection of success? Maybe. Are they designed to reflect how much you learned? Not necessarily. If you think about it, grades are designed to let you know how much you did not learn. In other words, how much you failed! You learn the material, take a test, and get a grade: A, B, C, D, F! If you get a letter grade of A, you are a genius and your parents pat you on your little head and say, "Great job!" If you get a letter grade of B, well, you are now "above average"; you are still pretty good, but not a genius; however, you are still a smart dude. Next, if you get a letter grade of C, you are "just an average Joe." Yes, you are in the middle of the pack, just like everyone else. At this point, you are not special anymore. A statistician would fit you nicely into the unrecognizable sixty-four percent of the population, right smack in the center of that famous bell shape curve, speaking statistically.

It only gets worse from here. If you get a letter grade of D, below standard equates to "depression," and even worse is receiving a letter grade of F. Receiving a poor grade implies you really did not learn anything and you are an utter "failure." Yes, you got it—F for Failure. At this point, your teacher and most of the student body views you as the dummy of the class. This is very sad. Our grading system is intended to convey how smart you are and how capable you can be; however, I am going to argue that this form of assessment is flawed and is not indicative of your abilities or knowledge, but rather provides a snapshot of what you learned or did not learn in a given moment in time.

Our current grading system does not really offer the opportunity to try different things and explore creative solutions to a problem. It is a one shot deal. You either learned it or did not. In many respects, this is perfectly acceptable; indeed, you need to learn certain tasks to be proficient in an area, but it also squelches creativity and discourages "thinking outside of the box." You do not want to take chances for fear of seeing that F for failure and being banished by the people of your tribe. This is why too many people embrace what is comfortable and safe and stop taking chances. They have learned that if they try something, there is a very good chance they will not succeed the first time. You hear them say, "Why try, because I am going to fail anyway."

This mindset does not convey the essence of what success really means or how you can become successful. Failure is not one option—failure is the only option! There is no such thing as an overnight success. You are not always privy to the long, arduous process that culminated in triumph. The process of what occurs behind the scenes is what needs to be taught and encouraged in the classroom.

The message should be: Who is willing to try the most times to achieve a goal or accomplish something? It should not be: Who can do it the best when the starting pistol fires? Allowing, and even encouraging, failure at the onset of a challenge will build a foundation of tenacity, exploration, and hope that the objective will someday be realized. Of course, we do not want to allow children to fail repeatedly without ever finding an answer, but we need to communicate to children and adults alike that learning is not a one shot deal. It is a process. How and what we learn from our "failures" is what makes us grow and develop. The people who are not allergic to both repeated failures and attempts are the ones who usually reap the greatest rewards. I know a chief operating officer of a company who told all of his directors that they do not fail nearly enough. They were too conservative and their fear of failing resulted in lackluster performance and a dearth of innovations.

I have heard of sales teams that give out awards to the person who makes the most calls to prospective customers.

Why would that be? This is because, as statistics suggest, the more customers called, the more sales will be closed, and the more sales that are closed, the more services are provided to customers, which of course generates more revenue. That is why it makes perfect sense to distribute awards to the person who has the fortitude to call on more customers, in spite of the many calls that are bound to result in failure.

Do not be afraid to try something, and then try something else, and keep trying until you get to where you want to go, what you want to do, or what you hope to acquire.

I came across many examples of this while viewing a YouTube video titled *Famous Failures*, citing twelve of the most successful people in recent history who were able to be considered the most "successful failures" in modern history. Consider the following:

- He was cut from his high school basketball team, went home, and locked himself in his room and cried. –Michael Jordan, six-time NBA champion, five-time NBA MVP, and four-time NBA All-Star
- He was not able to speak until he was four years old, and his teachers said he would "never amount to much of anything." –Albert Einstein, theoretical physicist & Nobel Prize winner
- She was demoted from her job as a news anchor because she "was not fit for television." –Oprah Winfrey, host of the multi-award winning talk show and possibly the most influential woman in the world
- He was fired from a newspaper for "lacking imagination" and "having no original ideas." –Walt Disney, creator of Mickey Mouse and winner of

twenty-two Academy Awards
- At age eleven, he was cut from his team after being diagnosed with human growth hormone deficiency, which made him smaller in stature than most kids his age. –Lionel Messi, three-time FIFA World Player of the Year
- After thirty years, he was left devastated and depressed after being unceremoniously removed from the company he started. –Steve Jobs, founder of Apple Inc. and co-founder of Pixar Animation Studios
- He was a high school dropout whose personal struggles with drugs and poverty culminated in an unsuccessful suicide attempt. –Eminem, thirteen-time Grammy Award winner, sold over ninety million albums worldwide
- A teacher told him that he was "too stupid to learn anything" and that he should go into a field where he "might succeed by virtue of his pleasant personality." –Thomas Edison, inventor of the incandescent light bulb
- They were rejected by Deca Recording Studios, who said, "We don't like their sound ... they have no future in show business." –The Beatles, the most commercially successful band and critically acclaimed band in history
- His first book was rejected by twenty-seven publishers. –Dr. Seuss, bestselling children's author
- His fiancé died, he failed in business, had a nervous breakdown, and was defeated in eight elections. –Abraham Lincoln, sixteenth president of the United States

In summary, the video asserts, "If you never failed, you never tried anything new. (Motivating Success, 2012)"

#3 Staying Composed in the Face of Adversity

We are still masters of our fate. We are still captains of our souls.
—Winston Churchill

Most people say that when the going gets tough, the tough get going. However, I believe when the going gets tough, the tough stay composed. Ben Roethlisberger, the quarterback for the Pittsburgh Steelers, is known as one of the most dangerous quarterbacks when his back is against the wall and his team is down a score at the end of the game. Known as Big Ben around the league, his uncanny ability to stay focused and maintain his composure in big games is so predictable that teams around the league know that they must play their best football at the end of a game, even if they are winning. Composure is one of the most important characteristics of a champion. Whether a person is a champion like Big Ben, or a top saleswoman on the verge of closing yet another sale, or a respected surgeon working to save the life of a patient, composure is a common thread among such diverse and accomplished professionals. Different circumstances yield unique problems, but you must be able to stay focused on the task at hand and avoid distractions from outside stimulus and from inside yourself. This skill can be learned.

Coaches are able to teach and train athletes to keep their composure when things go wrong. Unexpected predicaments invariably arise when you least expect them. Composure is essentially "distraction control" by not allowing unimportant factors to cloud your judgment, decision-making, and functioning. An article in the *Encyclopedia of Sport and Exercise Psychology* by Aidan Moran, and edited by Robert C. Eklund and Gershon Tenenbaum, describes how Bob Bowman, the coach of one of the world's greatest swimmers in history, Michael Phelps, introduced a variety of calamitous scenarios to Phelps during training swims. The purpose was to prepare him and give him the competitive advantage if something unexpected and unfavorable occurred in an actual competition. The article states that Bowman "… admitted to deliberately breaking Michael Phelps' goggles during practice so that he could learn to swim calmly without them, if necessary, in competition. Remarkably, this situation actually arose in the 2008 Olympics when Phelps won the 200-meter butterfly event, even though his goggles had been broken for the last 100 meters of the race."

This is a great example of how simulating an experience in a controlled environment can help you maintain your composure in the event that it does occur. Consider situations that may go awry and visualize the actions you could take to ameliorate a negative outcome. Is it a business meeting, an interview, a speech, or sporting event that you find yourself in that would need some "composure preparation"? If so, think of a worst-case scenario, then what you would do to combat an undesired result, just as Bowman did for Phelps. Preparing yourself in this manner will help you stay composed in a situation that may get hot and heavy.

CHAPTER 8

Building Internal Strength

A positive attitude may not solve all your problems, but it will annoy enough people to make it worth the effort.
—Herm Albright

Attitude: Your Attitude is Not Everything; It is the Only Thing

Charles Swindoll wrote an enlightened essay that encapsulates the whole notion of "attitude" more than anything that I have read.

"The longer I live, the more I realize the impact of attitude on life. Attitude to me is more important than facts. It is more important than the past, than education, than money, than circumstances, than failures, than successes, than what others think or say, or do. It is more important than appearance, giftedness, or skill. It will make or break a company, a church, a home. The remarkable thing is, we have a choice every day regarding the attitude we will embrace for that day. We cannot change our past. We cannot change the inevitable. The only thing we can do is play on the one string we have, and that is our attitude. I am convinced that life is ten percent what happens to me and ninety percent how I react to it. And so it is with you.

We are in charge of our attitude."

I think when Swindoll declares attitude "more important than facts," he is referring to positive energy. I'm sure you have been around someone who has a "good attitude." This person can uplift a room filled with negativity and shift the energy in the room so that it feels a little more optimistic. I also agree that attitude is truly more than facts, because the wrong attitude can make the data appear pretty dismal.

Swindoll alludes to the premise that you have total control of your attitude. You determine your attitude; it does not control you. When you have control over your attitude, you accept things as they are and are not likely to judge or color a situation with a negative brush stroke. Earlier in this book, I talked about the Force Field Analysis, where there are forces that are always opposed and fighting against each other. Accepting that there is a yin and yang in your life is the start of having a good attitude. Since they oppose one another, they can be viewed as positively charged and negatively charged. However, one side is not bad and the other side is not good. In most cases, we need both to stay in balance (remember homeostasis?).

A good example of this is the sodium and potassium balance, which is essential to keeping our biology in balance. The body needs the electrolyte minerals potassium and sodium to help make nerve and muscle cells work properly. The minerals work together to keep you in balance and keep your nervous system working in harmony. Sodium is primarily outside of body cells and more potassium concentration occurs inside cells, but both are found on each side of a cell wall. Deficiencies in either or both of these electrolytes may cause severe complications. If there is more sodium than potassium, the consequence is an imbalance in the blood and the body becomes out of balance. Complications associated with muscles and problems with the heart may arise; muscles in the body may cramp, feel weak or spasm; muscle fibers may also begin to break down and release protein into the blood, causing damage to the kidneys, just to name a few potential issues.

So, what does this balance of sodium and potassium have to do with attitude? People with positive attitudes tend to view the world the way it is and then choose a scenario that creates some semblance of balance. You could take the *attitude* and say that too much sodium is bad for you, which it certainly can be. Your sister could take the *attitude* and say that too much potassium is bad for you, which it certainly can be. Which one of you has a bad attitude? Look at both sides of the coin. A person with a good attitude would say that too much of anything is bad for you, but having the correct balance of both is the key to good health.

The essence of a positive attitude was clearly evident in my middle child following a soccer game in which his brother was played. After the game, my oldest was complaining and distressed that they lost the game. I am not sure if he was upset simply by the loss, or if it was the large margin by which the team lost. Nonetheless, he was visibly upset and talked about it on our way home in the car. I, of course, being the upbeat, "Oh, it's okay" father that I am, said, "It's okay to feel this way. You really want to give it your all again next time. There is only so much you can control. Learn from your mistakes ….," and basically all the stuff I've written about in this book. Of course, my pontificating was getting to be too much for a six-year-old and I lost him halfway through, I'm sure. As I was talking, though, the four-year-old chimed in and was able to sum up all that I was saying for the last ten minutes. He said, "Daddy, do you know what I do when I play soccer?"

I said, "What do you do when you play soccer?"

He said, "I try to be myself and never give up."

This sums up what it means to have a great attitude, and I sincerely doubt it can be said any more succinctly and earnestly than it was in that moment. My four-year-old taught me something that day. He reminded me that we must all trust in ourselves and believe in what we can do, and if we never give up, things will always turn out for the good. You might not win the game (whatever that game is for you), but you will walk away proud and feel successful that you always gave it your all and stayed true to yourself through the process. That is in the spirit of keeping a good attitude! Maybe the real lesson is to listen closely to the little ones. They come equipped with rose-colored glasses, innocence, trust, sincerity, and always seem to come up with the good stuff.

Perseverance: The Hard Work After Doing the Hard Work

The other day, as is a common occurrence in my house, my boys were wrestling with each other. After a while, Nathan, the oldest, said to his younger brother, Jacob, "I don't want to wrestle anymore." Jacob, of course, did not hear that. After about four exclamations from Nathan to his brother to stop his horsing around, Nathan finally came to me and said, "Daddy, tell Jacob to stop. I do not want to wrestle anymore."

Stoically, I said, "Jacob, please leave your brother alone." I went back to cooking dinner.

I then heard Nathan screaming, "Jacob, stop! I don't want to wrestle. Leave me alone." At this point, my wife admonished Jacob to leave his brother alone and to go play on his own.

Now I know that Jacob heard Nathan, his mother, and me say the same thing. Being a well-adjusted, active, fun loving three-year-old, he was well aware he did not want to be influenced by others. He stayed on task and true to his goal of engaging his brother in a wrestling match. He heard multiple commands to, "Leave your brother alone." Still, he chose not to take those suggestions from us. He did not respect his brother's wishes. He was having a darn good time wrestling with him. He persisted in wrestling with his brother even though Nathan was not interested.

While this could be construed in a negative light, I actually think more people should be like Jacob. I do not mean you should disrespect others' wishes and continue to bother people to the point of anger and frustration. What I am saying is that most of us are influenced by people's statements and can be redirected too easily and too quickly. How many times have you had a goal derailed by someone with just one statement? Many times, I have had people say, "You should not do that," or in a more subtle fashion, "Should you be doing that?"

There have been many occasions when I have taken a statement at face value and stopped what I was doing simply because I respected the person. The one thing I did not do is ask the question, "Why?" You cannot be afraid to dig a bit deeper. It may be better to listen to the rationale, carefully consider it, and then just keep on going, like Jacob. I believe this is the key to perseverance: to not respond to others too quickly or easily. I am not saying you should not listen and consider what is being said. What is being said can indeed be a good idea that could result in a positive outcome.

What I am trying to convey is the notion of superficially and acquiescently taking what is being said and abruptly stopping what you are trying to accomplish. At the risk of sounding negative, I am compelled to remind you that not all people may be on your team. You have to be smart enough and aware enough to know who is for you and who is against you. Unfortunately, this is just a reality. If you go back to the section on the "gravity of life," this is one of them. It also falls under Kurt Lewin's Force Field Analysis, where there are negative forces that hinder progress toward a goal. If you let people take you off course, you may languish there. If you let people keep you down, you will stay down. There are forces in play all the time. The one thing that you can do to negate those forces is to stay the course and not let others impede your progress. Just like Jacob, keep at it and keep wrestling, no matter what people say.

Discipline: Remember, Discipline Weighs Ounces, While Regret Weighs Tons

I recall a saying I heard years ago: "Discipline weighs ounces, while regret weighs tons." Out of all the characteristics needed to attain peak performance, the one that resonates is "discipline." Discipline is the force that says, "Do it now, even when you don't want to." Discipline is what Ben Disraeli called, "Consistency of purpose."

Setting a goal, staying focused, and continually taking action toward achieving that goal is discipline. Consistently accomplishing intermediate steps toward a worthy objective is discipline.

How do you acquire this phenomenon of discipline? Clearly, it is not going to knock on your door or fall from the sky. The only way to acquire discipline, like anything else, is to practice it. Decide on your goal, get active, and do something about it. Then do it again, and yet again, especially when you do not feel like doing it. The only way to become disciplined is by doing something you do not want to do. It is not easy, by any stretch of the imagination, but it is the most effective way to live and embrace a disciplined life.

The best advice I heard on this matter came from the great business philosopher, speaker, and writer, Jim Rohn, who said, "Don't wish it was easier; wish you were better." Once you start to practice the habit of discipline, it is like an infectious bug that lays its eggs into its host. Eventually, the eggs, one by one, start to hatch, and newborn bugs eventually seize control of the host. This is what happens when you decide to dedicate yourself to a goal. Discipline, as long as its host (you) feeds it, grows and eventually becomes part of your very being. This makes your tasks, projects, and behaviors become routine. Over time, discipline allows the behaviors you once had to become habit.

Doing something that you do not feel like doing is the most basic definition of discipline. A clear vision of the desired outcome can help you stay motivated. Indeed, the only way to consistently succeed is to set goals and exercise the necessary discipline to accomplish them. So many people who lack discipline find themselves falling short in attaining goals. You do not want to be a part of that group, do you?

One group who exemplifies the most persistent habit of discipline is the U.S. Navy SEALs. The concept of discipline was clearly featured in an article by Richard Feloni, writer for the *Business Insider*, which ran on yahoo.com, titled "Why this retired Navy SEAL commander has three alarm clocks and wakes up at 4:30 a.m." The article starts out by saying, "Retired Navy SEAL commander Jocko Willink has a habit of frequently tweeting out a photo of his watch when he's ready to take on the day. The watch face always reads somewhere around 4:30 a.m." Willink writes in his book *Extreme Ownership: How U.S. Navy SEALs Lead and Win*, "Discipline starts every day when the first alarm clock goes off in the morning. I say 'first alarm clock' because I have three, as I was taught by one of the most feared and respected instructors in SEAL training: one electric, one battery powered, one windup. That way, there is no excuse for not getting out of bed, especially with all that rests on that *decisive moment*." The article continues, "While waking up before anyone else had an advantage on the battlefield, there's no real need for Willink to get up at 4:30 anymore. However, he does so as a matter of principle, and it is why he has three alarms as a safeguard."

In my opinion, Willink explains the act of discipline most clearly when he proclaims, "The moment the alarm goes off is the first test; it sets the tone for the rest of the day. The test is not a complex one: when the alarm goes off, do you get up out of bed, or do you lie there in comfort and fall back to sleep? If you have the *discipline* to get out of bed, you win—you pass the test. If you are mentally weak for that moment and you let that weakness keep you in bed, you fail. Though it seems small, that weakness translates to more significant decisions. But if you exercise discipline, that too translates to more substantial elements of your life."

Pay close attention to his words, "If you get out of bed, you win—you pass the test." After reading this, I decided to set my alarm clock to wake half an hour earlier the next day. I did not go out and purchase two more clocks, like Willink, but at least I took the first step to introducing and practicing a new discipline. The point is that a little change in disciplined activity can produce big changes. You have the power to become disciplined. I hear people say, "I just don't have the willpower." If you say that right off the bat, you are giving up before you even start.

The only way to develop willpower is to practice discipline. Just because you set your alarm clock a half an hour earlier and did not get up when it rang does not mean you cannot keep trying. It takes practice. How many people do you know who try to lose weight and do not? "They say, "I just don't have the discipline." How about the people who are disciplined enough to lose twenty or thirty pounds only to gain it all back? Did they lose their discipline? Not really. They practiced discipline in the moment, because they, in fact, did lose the weight, but they did not build the habit of discipline.

Maintaining discipline for short periods is not that difficult. The problem is that people view discipline and willpower like holding their breath. You can hold your breath for a short time. Some can hold it longer than others, but eventually they will give up because they need the necessary oxygen to survive. You cannot hold it forever.

Discipline is not like holding your breath; it is more like brushing your teeth or taking a shower. Not many people miss those activities, right? I am sure you have taken a shower in the past twenty-four hours or will take one after you finish reading this book. Why do you brush your teeth and shower? Well, first you have to in order to be presentable and inoffensive at work in the morning. Second, you do it because it has become habit. Referring to brushing one's teeth and taking a shower every morning as being "disciplined" may sound almost absurd to most of you, but at some point in your life, it was a behavior that had to be taught and practiced until, eventually, it became a habit to which you give little thought.

If you partake in those activities every day and reap the rewards, then you can add a few important disciplines to your repertoire. How about exercising ten minutes a day, and couple that with ingesting two hundred fifty fewer calories per day (which, subsequently, equals a half pound of weight loss per week). Add ten more minutes of exercise and you will lose more. Cutting out two hundred fifty calories is only a couple of foods items per day. Over time, you will easily gain the discipline of those behaviors and you will be just like former U.S. Navy SEAL Jocko Willink, who awakes at 4:30 a.m. every morning on principle and feels like a winner every day he gets out of bed. Now *that* is the power of discipline!

I work with a woman who has been running for more than forty years. You might say that is impressive, which it certainly is, but you might also say thousands of people have been running for over four decades. However, this woman is a little different. The difference between these forty years is that she received a running journal as a Christmas gift in December 1979 and decided to set a goal to run every day for the next year. As it turns out, the goal of running three hundred sixty-five days in a row turned into running every day for the next thirty-seven years! Now, to her credit, she did disclose to me that she did not make it out to run for two of those days. I asked her why she missed those two days and she said, "I had an unexpected change in my routine and simply forgot."

Okay, missing two days out of thirteen thousand, five hundred and five is not bad. In April 2015, a hip injury plagued her and stopped her from running for three weeks. After healing from the injury, she was back on track and finished out the year 2015 not missing another day. This incredible feat of consistency is perhaps unmatched by all but the most avid runners. So, how is she able to do this day in and day out? I asked her about this and she replied, "I can't think of a reason not to run. I mean, if you are capable, there really is not a reason not to do it. It is much easier when you take away the option of not running." With this perspective, the discipline of running every day is unlikely to be dismissed and has attained the status of "habit." I guess we could all think of excuses not to run on a given day, but if you cannot think of a legitimate reason, then the only option is to run. This makes total sense if you plan to embark on a thirty-seven-year running streak.

I think the best description of discipline comes from management experts Jim Collins and Morton T. Hansen in their book *Great by Choice*. Collins and Hansen discuss discipline quite eloquently when they write, "Discipline, in essence, is consistency of action, consistency with values, consistency with long-term goals, consistency with performance standards, consistency of method, consistency over time. Discipline is not the same as regimentation. Discipline is not the same as measurement. Discipline is not the same as an article of obedience or adherence to bureaucratic rules. True discipline requires the independence of the mind to reject pressures to conform in ways incompatible with values, performance standards, and long-term aspirations. The only legitimate form of discipline is self-discipline, having the inner will to do whatever it takes to create a great outcome no matter how difficult."

Once you learn discipline, a type of momentum takes over and you find yourself gaining speed and acquiring more and more disciplined skills for future successes.

Momentum: Making Your Life Work for You

Professional hockey is one my favorite sports to watch. I am always amazed how quick, agile, and explosive the players are. They glide with the greatest of ease and can stop on a dime to control the puck, then pass it off with such precision that it connects to their teammate's stick as that person speeds gracefully toward the net. Do not blink, because you will miss a blinding bullet of a shot. The puck breezes smoothly in between the pads of the goaltender and a goal is scored. The excited voice of the announcer proclaims, "He shoots and scores!" What a great game.

What I find most interesting about the game of hockey is how the momentum can shift so rapidly. I watch as my team goes up by a point or two, playing well and settling comfortably into the pace of the game. They have command of the puck and control over the opposition. I am quite confident that my guys have the game in hand, but in an instant, the other team steals the puck, races down the ice, and dumps that little black biscuit into the net of my team. No more than a minute later, the other team scores again. All of a sudden, the other team is now handling the puck with ease, controlling it, passing it, shooting it, and doing so at will. I realize just how quickly the momentum shifted and I ponder why this happened.

I contemplate how the momentum could swing from one team to the other with just one move of the opposing player. How does this momentum take hold and continue to grow? We all notice this when it happens. It happens not only in sports, but also in business meetings. The negotiations are skewing one way and, all of a sudden, a person on the other side of the table says something that changes the perspective of the entire group, and quickly the *momentum* shifts to the other side of the table. So, just how do you create and sustain momentum?

First we will define momentum. Merriam-Webster's definition for the word "momentum" is, "The strength or force that allows something to continue or to grow stronger or faster as time passes." No matter what we are doing, be it playing a sport, conducting a business meeting, or negotiating a contract, a force will intensify as you fuel it with your energy.

I will apply a physical example to visualize momentum. Think about your car parked at the top of a hill. The brakes give out. What happens? Well, your vehicle starts to slowly roll down the hill and it begins to pick up more speed. The larger the vehicle, the slower the start, and the faster it will move down the hill, gaining more speed and power as it descends. If it reaches another hill at the bottom and does not have enough speed to crest that next hill, it will move up the hill for a short distance, run out of energy, and start to coast back down, landing in between the two hills. However, if your vehicle creates enough speed and energy, it will swoop down, then over that next hill to the other side. How does "the change of momentum" increase the speed and energy, and how does this relate to you?

First, you have to create enough energy to generate force and momentum. Invariably, you will meet resistance. We all do so in some shape or form; therefore, when embarking on a goal, you need to create enough momentum so that if and when you meet the resistance, you have enough psychic momentum to take you over that barrier. Without it, you will stall and find yourself like the car between the two hills. There is not enough energy to take you over to the other side. So the question is: How do we create and sustain momentum to get us to our goals and objectives?

There are three factors needed to set the momentum cycle in motion. The first is to take action; the second is to develop a strong desire; and the third is having faith that things will work out no matter what. I will explore these factors in more detail.

CHAPTER 9

Shut Up and Get to the Gym

Taking Action

During a meeting with a friend, I was describing my desire to write a book and explaining the obstacles I had already encountered, as well as those I was anticipating. He inquired as to when I planned to publish this book.

I replied simply, "Someday."

He looked me in the eye and admonished, "Someday is not a day of the week."

I asked him what he meant.

He replied, "I mean that you need to get off your ass, stop making excuses, set a date, and take action toward this project!"

While I contemplated a pithy response to his stern comment, he continued by saying, "The reason you are not making progress is pretty simple. You are not taking the action necessary to even get this book started. Also, you do not have a solid date in mind, and you are not really committed to the project—yet." Then he said something that I could not get out of my head for weeks. He said, "Don't say '*someday*,' say '*this*' day. That will make the difference between starting the job and eventually getting it done."

It is true; actions indeed speak louder than words. These were powerful words that impacted me greatly. I thought to myself, Why haven't I taken action yet? There were two reasons: pain and fear. What it comes down to is that your actions are handcuffed by the feeling of pain to take the action and the intense fear of failure.

Say you have to learn a new computer program for your job. You grumble, "Oh no … not another program to learn." Feeling incompetent and stupid before you even click to open the new program, you put it off and find something else to do; that is until the overwhelming fear rushes over you and you think, *Oh, no. If I do not learn it, I will be fired.* At that point, the feeling of losing your job trumps the feeling of not being able to learn the program. You quickly swallow your pride, take action, and ask your coworker for a few minutes of their time to help you learn the new system.

The fear of failure and the pain of the process are the two nemeses that can stop you from taking action. However, the opposite can happen if you start to take small actions, day by day. Momentum will start to surface and you get in the habit of doing. Confidence will build. Learning to take uncomfortable actions will become the "new normal" for you. As soon as you find yourself feeling scared, insecure, or uneasy, you will jump onto the task, knowing that everything will be fine. If you do fail, you will look at the failure as a success just because you tried. Taking the action was a success, no matter what the outcome. With this perspective, you cannot lose.

To get anything done, you have to take the action, have faith that the outcome will be in your favor. If you feel a little uncomfortable, this is the best time to move forward. This is the time where personal and professional growth is cultivated.

How to Become Stronger, Better, Faster

Currently, the top three killers in the United States are heart disease, cancer, and diabetes. Naturally, maintaining your physical health is paramount. If you define success by money, cars, houses, and trips around the world, none of it matters without the physical health to enjoy them. Physical health is something you can control, at least at the level of nutrition and conditioning. Your genetic predispositions are part of your makeup, but these can be influenced in part with how you behave, think, eat, and exercise. Making the right choices gives you a fighting chance to live a long, healthy, and fulfilling life. Often, it is our behavior and lack of discipline that causes the onset of poor health. The seemingly insignificant choices can yield significant consequences in the future.

In her book, *The DASH DIET Weight Loss Solution*, Marla Heller shares the results of her research when she writes, "Over sixty-seven percent of Americans are overweight or obese. And excess weight is not just a cosmetic problem." She goes on to say that health care costs for obesity hit $147 billion in 2008, which accounted for almost ten percent of the health care cost in the United States. According to Heller, "Someone who is obese spends $1,500 per year extra for medical care than someone of healthy weight." This is staggering. The resulting conditions that are a byproduct of obesity include hypertension (high blood pressure), type 2 diabetes, joint problems, sleep apnea, coronary heart disease, elevated cholesterol and triglycerides, certain types of cancer, stroke, gall bladder, and liver diseases. The good news is that choosing what to eat is all within your locus of control and can make a positive impact on your health in the short term and long term.

This relates to the advice offered by both my high school wrestling coach and my judo instructor, when we were training for competitions. They reminded me that I was the only one who could control how physically fit I was for the next match. I came to understand that my competitor may be more skilled, more knowledgeable, and more technically adroit than I was, but the one thing I could control was my overall conditioning, endurance, and strength. I owned those three things and had the power to do something about them. I knew my opponent was not going to warn me not to eat that donut since it could adversely impact my performance. I had to remind myself of the benefits of choosing the most nutritious food I could to give myself that physical edge to maximize performance. The things I chose to eat, the amount of rest and sleep I got, and the intensity, duration, and times I exercised were all under my control.

My days of formal competition have ended, but my coach's message continues to resonate with me, and, hopefully, it will resonate with you as well. Remember that your body is your temple. No one wants to live in a worn-down old woodshed. A strong wind will come along and blow the old thing away. This is very much like your body. You do not want disease to come along and bring you down. The best way to make sure that does not happen is for you to make sure your body is strong and healthy at the start; this way, if the winds of ill health one day blow your way, you stand a fighting chance.

Good health is one of the factors that need to be incorporated into the equation of success and happiness. Eating right and exercising is the simplest path to a healthier and better life. As always, see your doctor before starting any dietary and physical fitness program.

I Cannot Concentrate on Anything!

You are bombarded every day by TV, email, and social media posts of all kinds from Facebook to Twitter. The typical eighteen- to twenty-four-year-old exchanges one hundred nine text messages a day. That equates to a whopping three thousand two hundred per month, according to a Pew internet study. Other findings show that of the eighty-three percent of American adults who own cell phones, roughly seventy-three percent of them send text messages and about thirty-one percent of them prefer texting to actually talking on the phone.

It should come as no surprise that people rarely read past three sentences or that our ability to concentrate has been compromised. How about all the ads that Google+ and Yahoo post on the side of your screens? It is information overload. As I write this, I have no doubt that additional digital communication devices are being developed and placed on the market. The copious and clever mechanisms designed to derail your concentration have become a way of life in the twenty-first century.

Case in point, I have discovered long emails no longer work for me. Studies show that people rarely read emails containing four hundred words or more in totality. In fact, some people delete the message after reading only the subject line. Compare that with a book this size that has approximately fifty thousand words. Reading four hundred words in this book is .08 percent of its total. That translates into reading the table of contents.

Do you ever open your email and just give it a quick scan? If the material is more than three paragraphs, you most likely do your own word search to see if you notice anything that might be important for you to know and worthwhile reading. Can you identify? We do not really read anymore. We scan. I believe we have become a society of "scanners." We are barraged with so much information that we have adapted our reading skills to quickly scan the written word.

If you made it this far into this book, you are in a small percentage of the population. Congratulations! Acquiescing to the byproduct of rapid-fire media, I set this book up in a way for you to get information in bite-size pieces without needing to read a whole chapter that could take ten to twenty minutes. I mean, how are you going to read that much stuff while sitting at that red light? Oh, and by the way, if you are reading this section while you are driving, put your phone down until you have reached a complete stop! Thank you. Since the connection economy curtailed our attention span, I want you to be able jump up, flip to a section, read it quickly, get the idea, and mull it over briefly; then you can close the book to check the text message you just received. Go ahead and check the message now.

I am in no way opposed to our new means of communication. Actually, I love it, but I think we need to be cognizant about what we focus on and for how long. It is too easy to get caught up on the front page of Yahoo, where you are met with a multitude of teasers, and before you know it, forty-five minutes have gone by and you have not done a thing but learned which celebrities are getting divorced.

In reality, your ability to concentrate is not necessarily compromised; the problem is the subject matter on which you concentrate. You can let the information control you or you can seize control of the information. Doing so takes focus, self-control, and conscious thought. You should not allow yourself to succumb to the Pavlovian response of the bell ringing and the dog salivating (or the modern equivalent: the phone dinging and the person reaching for it). I strongly feel that to really experience a peak performance lifestyle, you must learn to live in the modern world with a "conscious concentration." Rather than being conditioned to reach for the phone following the ding, condition yourself to ask the question: Do I really need to check that now?

Conscious concentration is a way of deciding how to respond and when, and to break free of the constant need to read and respond to email, text, and whatever is stealing your attention and concentration. The next time your phone dings and you receive a text, wait five minutes before you check it. I know it will be difficult, but give it a try and force yourself to continue to do what you were doing before hearing that *ding* of temptation. This will make a difference in your life.

CHAPTER 10

If at First You Don't Succeed, Don't Come Back Home

On the wall outside of the room where my high school wrestling team practiced hung a poster that said:

Good, Better, Best

Never let them rest

Until good is better and better is best.

This little poem is obviously about striving for improvement. I always thought of this poem as trying to "one up" yourself day in and day out. The Japanese call it Kaizen. It is the constancy of a quality and improvement process. The notion is to continually improve your position. The United States Navy SEALs teams have a great mantra for self-improvement, which is the cornerstone of their culture and training: *The only easy day was yesterday.* It begs for anyone who thinks they worked hard today to just wait until tomorrow! If you want to perform at an elite level in any field of endeavor, your mindset should always be to prepare for the challenges you may face in the future and to meet them in a productive and effective manner.

Remember gravity? It is always pulling on you. Since gravity is pulling you down, you will need strength to move upward. That is where goals come into play. Setting a goal helps you establish, and ultimately improve, your current status or position. Improving your position means getting better at what you are doing, gaining more skills, and taking the steps necessary to reach your ultimate goal. One problem is that most people do not know how to go about setting goals. You may have been advised, as I was, to simply "set a goal" and that was it, with no explanation of how or why. Therein lies the first quandary, and it lends itself to the reason so many people set goals they have little chance of attaining.

The promising news is that there are people who routinely define goals and are able to achieve them on a consistent basis. I learned and established a well-defined system for setting goals. I have heard people say, "I don't have the discipline to reach my goals," but in reality, this is not why people fail. More often, the inability to achieve a goal has to do with the absence of a definitive system or plan for its attainment. Do not get me wrong; discipline is also important. You must possess discipline to get things done. However, once you have an effective system in place, the system allows you to create habits, which ultimately results in reaching your goal. Laying out a plan, staying true to the plan, and, if necessary, improving that plan are the keys to success.

Winners Expect to Get Hit and They Like It

If you want to enjoy the rainbow, be prepared to endure the storm.
—Warren Wendel Wiersbe

Winners expect to get hit ... and they like it. To be a winner, you must ready yourself for the impact, and afterwards, move forward with a smile on your face. It has been said that *the more successful you become, the more criticism you receive, the more suspicious people become of you, and the less they trust you.* You must be ready to get bounced around, challenged, and beaten up. You will be tried at the mental, emotional, spiritual, and physical level. If you are not being criticized or questioned, you may be playing the game too safely. You might not realize your full potential if you attach too much significance to what others are telling you.

I will draw this parallel for you. Imagine a running back in a professional football game who is not willing to get hit. How many yards would that player accumulate during a game? Not many, for sure. Running backs are conditioned to run toward and through large, angry men. They have to be tough and must relish the punishing physicality of the game. Their job is to run toward a bunch of giant men whose goal is to create an impenetrable brick wall between the runner and the goal line. Taking an almost masochistic pleasure in the hits, the running back rushes the line, getting battered, smashed, pressed, and abused each time he is given the ball. He endures this "abuse," while showcasing his determination, adroitness, and skill. This is all in an effort to achieve that all-important "W" when the final gun sounds. What a job!

This is not so different from what you should experience when you set your goals and plan in motion. Set your goal and wait for the hit. Invariably, someone or something will step in the way and knock you off kilter. But wait! It could get even worse. Others may use aversive psychology to make you feel bad and uncomfortable, leading you to question yourself and your motives. Those who are determined to see you fail may even threaten you in some manner if you continue to pursue your endeavor. I wish I could tell you that the more successful you become the easier it will get, but that is simply not true. What I can say is that if you hang in there, stick with the plan, and slowly and methodically continue to chug along, you will eventually come out the other end just like the running back as he forces his way through the wall of the defense. A hole opens up, the field becomes an expansive sea of green, and all he sees is the goal line awaiting his plunge to victory. So, stay in the game, plan to get hit, and keep fighting until you see your goals manifest themselves right before your eyes.

PART 3

Putting it all Together and Coming out on Top

CHAPTER 11

The Seven Things You Should do Every Day

The three great essentials to achieve anything worthwhile are, first, hard work; second, stick-to-itiveness; third, common sense.
—Thomas Edison

All great athletes, leaders, businesswomen and men, doctors, lawyers, CEOs, engineers, legislators, civic leaders, teachers, parents, astronauts, our men and women serving in the armed forces, high school and college students, and anyone else like you find themselves performing some task or developing some type of talent on a daily basis. So, why do some people succeed and others fail? Why do some athletes keep working to perfect their craft and others quit? Why do some students stay in school while others drop out? Why do some parents become frustrated with their children and others deal with an issue and move on?

As you recall from the first two parts of this book, there are things you can control and others you cannot. There are beliefs that are self-limiting and self-imposed that you can change. These factors can affect your mind, emotions, and performance. Since you know that there are things you can and cannot control, the question is: What is the formula that can help you succeed and lead and help others to be better than you are today? What can bring you to the level of success, happiness, and value you are striving for in your life?

I believe there are seven simple actions you need to perform on a daily basis to find the consistency of success you seek. They are called the Super Seven of Success. These are seven steps you need to take to attain your goals. If you employ these strategies on a daily basis, you will become who you want to be and acquire what you want to possess.

In Part 1 of this book, you learned various factors that may be preventing you from going forward. In Part 2, you started to build a foundation for your success. Now, in Part 3, we will focus on the seven actions that successful people and leaders develop, practice, and flawlessly execute.

The Super Seven are as follows:
1. Commitment
2. Goals
3. Focus
4. Self-Talk
5. Imagery
6. Mental Rehearsal
7. Simulation

Imagine white light moving through a prism and being refracted into six colors; so, too, are the actions of your life. Steadfast commitment is that beacon of white light needed to drive your success. Once you make that commitment, six tools are spawned to make that commitment a reality. Your commitment is the white light holding all the colors of the visual spectrum. Once you make the commitment, the light refracts into six colors, vividly displayed as the tools needed to make that commitment real. Once you make a commitment, you then set goals, establish focus, create positive energy through self-talk, and form a clear image as you envision the desired outcome in your mind. You rehearse the behaviors needed to acquire the skills to meet your challenge and to take you to an optimal performance. You experience success, happiness, and you find yourself living in the zone more consistently than ever before. Now we will get started on the first success principle: commitment.

CHAPTER 12

Commitment: You are Either in or You are Out

Unless commitment is made, there are only promises and hopes, but not plans.
—Peter Drucker, professor, manager, business consultant

What is the one foundation strong enough to hold the pillars of success? What is the very cornerstone of success? What is the primary attribute among all others that makes the difference between success and failure? Is it talent and intelligence? Is it education and erudition?

This is the one misconception that many people have regarding success. It is not who you know or what you have; success is based on one thing and one thing only, and that is commitment. Commitment is at the very core of success. Success is not a birthright of the most talented, the most attractive, or the brightest and the best among us. The successful person is the one who has the unfettering commitment to a purpose. It is the person who does not ever give up on what they want. It is the one who says with conviction, "It is not a matter of *if*; it is a matter of *when*." The difference between success and failure does not rest on talent, skill, or ability. Commitment to a goal, an objective, a mission, or a purpose is the difference between being a winner or a loser.

The Commitment Highway

Your path to commitment is likely to diverge at some point, and when it does, you will either commit or acquiesce. Remaining true to your commitment will result in the changes in your life you desire. Acquiescing will result in stagnation.

Commitment is a process, and completing the steps in this process is essential to realizing success. First, you must have a clear awareness and understanding of what you want. Clarity and vision are integral parts of the process. Not having a clear understanding of what you want is like hopping in the car with no real destination in mind. If there is no understanding or awareness of what you want to accomplish or where you want to be at journey's end, you are likely to remain mired in your present state and unwilling to make the commitment necessary to move forward. With no awareness and understanding, you are likely to wander aimlessly along the path to commitment.

If you do not have a clear understanding of exactly what you want to achieve, your mind goes into a holding pattern by resisting the need to commit. Think of the cliff divers in Mexico. What greater commitment can there be than taking a plunge off a thirty-foot high cliff? However, if they're standing at the edge uncertain if the water is deep enough or if there are jagged rocks below the surface, they probably should hold off on committing to the dive. So, delaying commitment for the right reason is not a bad thing if you are doing it because you do not have adequate information to confidently move forward with your plan. The prospect of change is wed to uncertainty, and for many people, the ensuing desire to avoid it at all cost.

With this feeling of uncertainty comes resistance, and your resistance is a defense mechanism that protects you from failure or being hurt in some way; therefore, it hinders your ability to make a commitment. The good news is that if you are feeling like you are resisting the commitment, then you are still giving energy to it. With energy comes the desire for greater understanding and additional information you may need to move to the next step in the commitment process. This information will take the form of why, what, when, who, and how? Once you gather this information, you will gain the confidence needed to make that commitment and the belief that your commitment is profitable. This is only possible when you develop a keen sense of awareness and understanding. Only then can you commit to the endeavor of your choice without reservation.

10 Commandments to Commitment

Thou shalt BELIEVE IN THE COMMITMENT.

Belief is the start of all committed action. Without truly believing in your causes, projects, and goals, there is no way to reach excellence. The internal drive to find the passion and commitment is one that is of value to yourself, which is the genesis of believing you will be extraordinary. Belief is the cornerstone to excellence. And if belief is the cornerstone, then faith is the foundation that is essential to all commitments. Deep faith in your ideals will keep you grounded and committed when things are difficult and dark. This is the real secret to success. How long it takes to reach your goals is insignificant; if you keep moving forward to your goals, believing in yourself and keeping the faith, it will all work out in the end. Since commitment is not a spectator sport, you must take the third step: action. To keep the momentum, action needs to be taken on a consistent basis. The unwavering belief, stanch faith, and consistent action, taken under any circumstances, will manifest the behaviors of the truly committed. That is what is called the ecology of commitment: belief, faith, and action.

Thou shalt WANT IT MORE.

Those considered successful always "wanted it more," "gave the extra effort," and "gave it their all." There is no free lunch. You need a certain grit to stick with something. Things will get difficult and that must be expected. It is easy to start something, but much harder to stay with it to the end. You know the old saying, "When the going gets tough, the tough get going." Trite but true. Desire comes from within. It is you saying, "This is going to happen, come hell or high water, and nothing will stop me from trying." Remember what Jim Rohn's mentor said to him when he was having trouble in his life? He admonished, "Don't wish it was easier; wish you were better. Don't wish for less problems, wish for more skills." There is wisdom in those two sentences and a good philosophy to draw upon when things get difficult and you need a little bit more grit to keep going.

Thou shalt HAVE THE DESIRE to succeed.

Desire is the fire that burns within you. Desire can range from a candle flame to a raging bonfire. The intensity of that fire drives you to produce results. The larger the fire you have in you, the more desire and motivation to take any project to its completion. Without a burning desire, your motivation is cold and lifeless and you lack the energy and passion to do anything, and in time, the commitment will die. Often, it is not the best athlete who wins the gold; it is the one with that inextinguishable flame.

Thou shalt be the MASTER OF SKILL.

Desire and vision are certainly key elements to a committed action, but without skills, you will not have the tools necessary to succeed. Think of it this way. Your car breaks down. Since you want your car to start working again, you look under the hood to see what is wrong. Now, if you are like me and have limited skill in the area, you cannot identify or fix the problem. Your car sits there until a tow truck arrives to take it to the garage where there are certified technicians who have the skills to diagnosis the problem and fix it. However, what if you get a flat tire? This might be different for you. You know what the problem is and you are motivated to fix it so you can get to where you are going. You open your trunk, pull out the jack and spare tire, jack up the car, and change the tire. You can see by these two examples that wanting something and having the desire are not enough. You must possess or develop the skills necessary to accomplish your objectives. Many people say they are committed to a goal and have the desire to commit to the action, but then fail to realize that they do not have the necessary skills to accomplish their goal. They find themselves in a vicious cycle of committing, failing, and then simply quitting. This is not from a lack of trying or committing to a task, but rather the absence of skills necessary to get the job done. They keep trying and failing before coming to the realization they are not proficient in a certain area. To recognize that your commitment is wavering simply because you do not possess a certain skill is an important step. You may need to do some growing, acquire skills, and adjust your goals in a realistic venture. You may need others to assist you in the learning process and to help you maintain the level of commitment you need to realize your goals.

Thou shalt LEARN FROM OTHERS.

Currently seven billion people are in the world and it continues to grow. Every year, 187,000 books are published. An internet search will find you almost anything generated by people around the world. Many people can help. Anyone who is committed to a goal must be equally committed to learning. Learning from others is the fastest way to success. This formula is simple: Identify the people who have already succeeded in your area of interest, figure out how they did it, and model that process. More often than not, you will pick up techniques and strategies that you can adopt in some shape or form. Be a sponge for knowledge. Do not be afraid to ask for help or an explanation. The more questions you ask, the more you will learn. In this era of technology, the answers are at our fingertips and can be accessed with just a few key strokes.

Thou shalt BE SELF-MOTIVATED.

You cannot expect commitment to originate from others. Commitment requires self-motivation. Can someone else motivate you? Not really. Perhaps someone can kindle that fire of motivation and desire, but it cannot be sustained without self-motivation. Self-motivation stems from positive self-talk and vision. No one can think for you and no one else can lay claim to your goals. Repeat your positive affirmations day in and day out to stay on course and committed toward your endeavors.

Thou shalt CONSTANTLY FIND NEW WAYS TO IMPROVE.

Commitment is not a stagnant phenomenon. It is a fluid action that requires learning that, in turn, produces improvement. Committed people always find ways to improve themselves through study and learning. Think about those little toys that you wind up with a key to propel the toy forward. These toys rely exclusively on windup power and clockwork mechanisms rather than electricity or batteries. Now envision that same type of mechanism generating the energy of your commitment. The more you turn that key, the more energy you give to your efforts of reaching your goal. You can wind it up as tightly as the mechanism allows, giving it all the energy it can possibly store. Once you let it go, it scuttles across the floor but eventually runs into a wall. It just keeps bumping into that wall until it eventually runs out of energy and stops. It cannot readjust, turn around, and totter off in a different direction. It cannot learn and adjust to its environment. Extend this to yourself. You can wind yourself all up, commit to something and march toward your goals, but be prepared to bump up against a few walls along the way. If you don't adjust and take the necessary steps to get around or over those walls, you may find yourself running out of energy like that little toy. Proverbially speaking, you don't want to "keep banging your head against the wall."

Thou shalt BE SUPPORTED IN THEIR ENDEAVORS.

You've heard the saying, "You are what you eat," right? Well, here is another one: *You are who your friends are.* Committed people surround themselves with people who support their efforts. Like viruses, behaviors are contagious. If you are around people with runny noses who are coughing and sneezing, there is a good chance that you will pick up the same common cold they have and you will start coughing, sneezing, and your nose will run. Similarly, if you surround yourself with others who have not only set goals, but have seen them through to fruition, you are likely to stay true to your own endeavors. Rather than sharing germs, they will share their own trials and tribulations and help you gain the fortitude you will need to see your own vision become a reality.

Thou shalt BE KEENLY AWARE OF THE CHANGING ENVIRONMENT.

The only constant in life is change. Currently, technology changes every three to six months. Computers double their memory capacity every two years. More and more automobiles are now powered by electricity instead of petroleum. It is now a world economy rather than a national economy. The world is getting smaller with the capacity to connect to each other. The accessibility to gain knowledge and experiences expands outward. This can be both scary and exciting. To deal with this fast-paced, evolving environment, you need to be adroit, adept, and agile in your awareness, your assessment, and your actions.

Thou shalt BE TENACIOUS.

If there is one word that is the underlying partner to commitment, it is tenacity. One definition of tenacious is "The quality or fact of being able to grip something firmly. Or the quality or fact of being very determined." There is a plethora of words commonly associated with the word tenacious, including persistence, determination, perseverance, doggedness, strength of purpose, tirelessness, indefatigability, resolution, resoluteness, resolve, firmness, patience, purposefulness, staunchness, steadfastness, staying power, endurance, stamina, stubbornness, intransigence, obstinacy, pertinacity, and my personal favorite—obduracy.

However, two of the more descriptive terms used to define tenacious are "grip firmly" and "determined." These embody the whole notion of commitment: grabbing onto something you want with steadfast determination no matter how difficult the situation becomes. You will inevitably encounter obstacles along the way, so expect these difficulties and embrace them, because in the long run, they will help you grow. Tenacity requires you to hang on; and, if, or when, you fall off of that horse, make sure you pick yourself up, jump back in that saddle, and keep riding to your goal! Commitment means never giving up on your goals. So, keep learning, trying, and maintaining that grip and, eventually, you will succeed.

A Little Secret to Commitment: Do not Quit!

Derek Redmond was favored to win the Olympic medal in the 400-meter sprint in the 1992 Barcelona Olympic Games. Just 150 meters into the race, Derek felt a searing pain in his right leg. In agony, he fell to the ground with a torn hamstring. Determined to finish the race, Derek hopped as fast as he could around the track. Suddenly, a man broke through security, wrapped his arm around Derek's shoulder, and grabbed his arm to offer assistance. This man was his father. "You don't have to do this," he told his son. "Yes, I do," Derek replied. "Well, then, we're going to finish this together!" Shortly before the finish line, Derek's father let him go to complete the race under his own power. Derek received a standing ovation from a crowd of over sixty-five thousand people. The moment was captured in the media with the accompanying clip, affirming, "When you don't give up, YOU CANNOT FAIL!"

If quitters never win and winners never quit, how can you even consider quitting if you are serious about success? To improve upon anything in your life, you cannot afford to quit. If you are trying to lose weight and "improve your health," and your goal is to lose twenty pounds, do you get to ten pounds and say, "I'm done"? Of course, it is good if you lose the ten pounds and keep it off and maintain a reasonably healthy regimen of diet and exercise. Ten pounds is not bad; as a matter of fact, ten pounds is good. However, you have to ask yourself why you did not continue working toward your original goal of losing twenty pounds.

Perhaps you bailed out at ten pounds for many reasons that made sense to you at the time. Maybe it was too hard, or you got tired, or the kid's baseball schedule changed and it interfered with your exercise time. Whatever it was, it is the quitting that is of concern. Excuses can be your best friends when you want to stop something that is difficult. They are certainly not in short supply and are quite convenient to pull out when you hit a sticking point. In his book *The Dip*, Seth Godin talks about how there is a dip in any process, venture, or goal, and that it usually comes when people just stop what they are doing and move on to something else. Failure thirstily waits when you do not push past that dip.

In his book, Godin describes a well-reported study of salespeople who quit after the fifth contact with a prospect. "After five times, the salesperson figures she's wasting her time and the prospect's, so she quits and moves on." The study reports that customers buy on the seventh try eighty percent of the time.

Jack Canfield, the author of *Chicken Soup for the Soul*, was turned down by more than one hundred fifty publishers before one of them agreed to publish his book. Now the book has sold over five hundred million copies worldwide, has been translated into forty-three languages, and published in more than one hundred countries. With more than two hundred fifty titles, the *Chicken Soup for the Soul* series of books has sold more than one hundred ten million copies in the United States and Canada, with retail sales exceeding one hundred million dollars per year. This is a great example of Canfield's persistence and commitment to make this book the great success that it has become.

So, keep trying. Just remember, great things usually do not work out on the first, second, or even the third try. As it turns out, the third time is not necessarily a charm, but perhaps the seventh time is. Stay true to your dreams and goals—and keep trying!

CHAPTER 13

Goals: Being Better than You Were Yesterday

Every day you may make progress. Every step may be fruitful. Yet there will stretch out before you an ever-lengthening, ever-ascending, ever-improving path. You know you will never get to the end of the journey. But this, so far from discouraging, only adds to the joy and glory of the climb.

—Winston Churchill

I gave a presentation to associates from a large insurance agency about setting goals, among other things. I opened the talk by saying, "I weep at the notion of goal setting and never really believed in it." At that point, the regional sales manager, who invited me to speak, sank down in his chair as if to say, "Oh no, why did I invite this guy to talk to my people?" In time, it became clear why I opened with this. First, I do believe we throw around the word "goals" quite frequently, without really giving pause to its meaning. Second, I believe that people set their goals without giving them the daily credence they deserve, too often resulting in failure to attain them.

Once you have a clear vision of your future, you need to create a pathway to get there. Visualization is the picture you paint for yourself. It is the motif of your life, and it is your goals and objectives that color it. You cannot underestimate the power of setting goals. You can dream all you want, but without clearly defined measurable goals, you will be swayed off course by the strong winds of life. Emerson said, "We aim above the mark to hit the mark."

Many people wish for a specific outcome, but many do not ever reach their goals. You cannot reach a goal that you cannot see any more than you can hit a target you do not have. Clearly defining and producing images gives you the ability to make the invisible visible. You are the producer of your life, determining the scenarios, environments, places, or anything you incorporate in the show. You set the stage and focus on the process. Think what you will be contributing and what you will offer. Do not worry about what others think or say and stay focused on why you are here and what you want to do.

Of course, like many things in life, this is easier said than done. It is so easy to begin the day with lofty ambitions and the best intentions of progressing toward our goals. Then, before we know it, it is 10:00 p.m. and another day has slipped by. Most of us live busy lives, so you must find creative ways to squeeze in the time to capture your ideas and dreams.

If you are like most people, you spend hours in the car, on a bus, in a subway, or in the air flying from city to city. Let us take John, for example. He wakes up in the morning, showers and shaves, drinks a cup of coffee, makes breakfast, and is out the door to work. He lives in the suburbs and travels an hour to his office in the city.

During his drive, he is free to think about anything he wants, and does so on the way home as well. He has a CD player, radio, cell phone with internet access, email, and everything else he could possibly need on his commute. Like most people, he listens to the radio and checks his text messages and email at red lights, all the while thinking about, well ... nothing important. Nevertheless, something changed one day with John. He starts to think about how much time is wasted traveling to and from his job. Two hours a day of commuting equates to ten hours of travel each week, which calculates to forty hours a month, which comes out to a grand total of four hundred eighty hours a year! Therefore, he spends four hundred eighty hours a year listening to the radio, checking text messages and emails on his phone, and listening to talk radio and hit songs from Kelly Clarkson, Lady Gaga, Maroon 5, among others.

John finally realizes that his commutes are pretty enjoyable, but he's wasting four hundred eighty hours of thinking about nothing, like part of his life is being flushed down the toilet. John feels that he is so busy that he does not have enough time to pursue what he really wants. John works in insurance but is interested in advertising and dreams about starting a small advertising agency. He doesn't think he has the time to sit down and map out his plan by thinking creatively about his dream and clearly defining the steps he needs to make it real. He knows that working hard and taking care of the family is his primary responsibility, so finding uninterrupted time to design an actual plan is challenging. Where could he find that *creative thinking time*?

When asked the best place to think, he responds, "The best place to think is in the shower. That time in the morning is my jump-start time. I come up with ideas in the shower." We all do, but John does something more. He keeps a journal close at hand so if a great idea pops into his head, he writes it down before it disappears into the cosmos. He also recognizes the glut of valuable time he has traveling to and from work. He decides he will not listen to the radio, play his favorite CD, or check his messages on his phone while driving to his job. In the silence, he will think—and think a lot.

He explains, "Think about it; when do you actually have two hours a day to just think, uninterrupted? No one asks you to take out the trash, kids aren't asking for a drink of water, and all the other things that interrupt the creative thinking process." So how does he capture his great ideas and plans for the advertising agency while speeding down the interstate at sixty-seven miles an hour? John simply dictates his ideas into his phone. While it seems technology is often the culprit in making our lives so frenzied, in this case, it is a forerunner to the realization of a dream.

You Cannot Manage What You do not Measure

There are many models for setting and achieving goals, so the purpose of this book is not to reinvent the wheel but to introduce a system that I feel is effective for achieving, succeeding, and reaching your goals. The model I present here is one that I learned years ago and have since used with great success.

7-Step Goal Setting Process:

1. Brainstorm ideas: write down as many as you can think of
2. Mark off goals that are unrealistic or unattainable (at this present time)
3. Separate your goals into short-range objectives and long-range goals
4. Stack the *whys* you want this goal
5. Put a date on your goal
6. Create a source list
7. Write a plan of action and record your progress

Before beginning, you need to have a keen understanding of what constitutes a goal, why you should set a goal, and the steps involved in doing so. This system will also teach you how to evaluate your progress, and, finally, when you have reached your goals, why it is important to celebrate your success. I will teach you to create in your mind what you really want so that you can then direct, organize, and implement an effective plan of action to achieve that vision.

This process can be used for two levels of goal setting: life planning and specific target planning. Life planning involves all aspects of your life, including physical and mental aspects as well as social and economic aspects. The other is your specific target plan, which has stricter parameters. When using your specific target planning, you take a specific aspect of your life and set goals that are geared toward achievement in that area. So, before you start the first phase of goal setting, decide whether you will be working on a life plan or a specific target plan.

Goal setting requires you to be actively involved and invested in defining and acting upon your goals, mentally and physically, every day. You can have the best model and plan, but if you do not give some attention to attaining your goal on a daily basis, you will most likely find your resolve weakening, thereby diminishing your chances for success.

No, Seriously, What Are Goals?

So, what are goals and why are they valuable? Goals are the futuristic landmarks, accomplishments, and achievements one sets for oneself. Goals are the future. With a solid goal, you can ultimately predict the future by creating it. Your vision of the future and your current reality merge into one as you see your goals accomplished.

The value of a goal is that it serves as the impetus that drives you toward your dreams. Goals give you purpose, hope, and possibilities. They are valued because they give you a sense of mission and a purpose in life. Without them, it is like getting out of bed in the middle of the night without turning on a light. You bump around, feeling the walls, trying to get a sense of where you are in the room, all the while tripping over stuff. In contrast, you could simply turn on the light and walk safely out of the room. Having a clear goal is not so different. Without a goal, you cannot see where you are going or envision what you want. With a goal, you can have a vivid picture of where you are heading.

Step 1: Brainstorming Ideas!

Brainstorming ignites cognitive sparks, which produce a collection of ideas that lead to feelings of inspiration, motivation, and vision. Brainstorming begins the passionate blaze of desire that, when followed, produces champions. It is the motivation to take on the challenges that lie ahead. It is your vision of the future. Brainstorming manifests possibilities and directs focus. It is a way to collect ideas to create something significant and pleasurable as you traverse your life path.

How to do you go about brainstorming? If you are target planning, you must first make a list of everything you want or anything that relates to the specific target. If you are life planning, you should write whatever comes to your mind, no matter how ridiculous these thoughts might seem. While brainstorming, let go of all your inhibitions and let your thoughts run wild.

Remember the story of the genie in the bottle? The man finds the bottle, rubs it, and a genie pops out and says to the man, "I can grant you three wishes." The man wishes, but he only wishes for one thing instead of three. His one wish was to grant himself all the wishes needed for the rest of his life. Start to brainstorm by thinking of anything and everything you ever wanted, such as ...

1. Where do I want to go?
2. What do I want to do?
3. How do I want to be?
4. What do I want to make?
5. Whom do I want to see?
6. What do I want to have?
7. Who do I want to become?

As you consider these questions, take fifteen minutes and write no less than fifty things on a sheet of paper, or better yet, in a journal. Just write and keep writing. The key is to write it down and keep it visible. There is something magical about seeing the goal on paper. Print or handwrite your goals instead of typing them. Make it personal. Own it. Once you've completed this step, move on to the second step, which is determining if the goals are feasible.

Step 2: Realistic and Attainable Goals

At this point in the process, you need to decide which of the items you wrote on paper are realistic and attainable. I know what you are saying: "Dave, you just had me write everything I ever wanted in life and now you are telling me to earmark only those that are realistic?" Yes. You have it! It is wonderful to dream big, but you also do not want to trip on the first step of your journey and fall flat on your face. Some of your more lofty goals may inspire you and lead you to accomplish other goals toward that end; however, there are also goals that are merely pipe dreams that will be a waste of your time.

Let me give you two ways to know whether your goals are unrealistic or unattainable. First, if you are completely devoid of skills needed for a particular goal, in all likelihood, it is unattainable. Imagine you wanted to be an Olympic figure skater in the next Olympic Games but you do not know how to skate. This would be a good example of setting a goal that is totally out of your field. But be careful. Some goals may not be attainable at this time, but you do not know about the future. Imagine that you are eight years old and your goal is to become an

Olympic figure skating champion in your twenties. This would definitely be a worthy goal because you would have the time to develop the skills necessary to make your dreams a reality.

Second, a goal is unattainable if you have to depend on luck to achieve it. For example, you are going to set a goal to make two million dollars. However, your plan is to play the lottery to acquire this money. Yes, you have a goal and you have a plan, but you have no control over which numbers pop up in the machine. Your success rate will be low because you have to depend on luck to win the money. Actually, your odds of being struck by lightning are greater than winning the lottery.

While you have no control over your luck, you have complete control over the effort you put into reaching a goal, and your success toward that end is dependent on how hard you are willing to work for it. Even if we do not reach some of the goals we set for ourselves, striving toward them and focusing on them vastly improves our lives. This process of self-improvement ultimately takes us to a higher level of consciousness, expands our abilities, and brings other goals within reach.

If the goals on your list are outside of your current realm, or if luck is the only way to attain them, then you must discard them. When you do this, remember that some goals may be unrealistic now, but they may become viable with some growth. Now, review your brainstorming wish list and choose the goals you think are currently attainable.

Step 3: Connecting the Dots: Short-Range and Long-Range Goals

It is better to take many small steps in the right direction than to make a great leap forward only to stumble backward.

—Old Chinese Proverb

The prospect of running a marathon may seem staggering; however, if you devise a plan with short-term objectives, the goal becomes quite reasonable. It is a matter of developing a training schedule that incorporates increasingly longer runs every week until you have acquired the skill and conditioning needed to tackle twenty-six miles. Completing your weekly miles leading to the race is a series of short-range goals. Once you toe the starting line at the race, you should continue to incorporate short-term objectives by focusing only on the mile immediately ahead, knowing that this will lead you to your ultimate goal of completing the race. When you are developing a goal plan, write down the specific steps you need to take, the criteria for success at each level, and a time frame for completing them. This helps you stay on course and allows you to celebrate smaller victories en route to your final destination.

Step 4: Ask Why You Want This Goal

Determining the reason for setting a particular goal is critical in deciding how to go about accomplishing it. If you decide your goal is to become a millionaire, ask yourself why. If you want to use that money to travel, perhaps that can be accomplished in a variety of ways, such as becoming a travel agent, an airline pilot, or joining the Navy. If you are thinking you would use that money to purchase a nice car (or several), maybe you should pursue a career in car sales as you squirrel away money from your salary in a car fund. If you want that amount of money for the security and status it affords, that is fine too. Your plan to acquire it should reflect that. Just remember that answering the *why* may help you determine if this is a goal that is worthy of your time and effort.

Step 5: Put a Date on Your Goal and Prioritize

By now, you may have whittled down your list from your brainstorming session to several long-range goals. Now you need to decide which one to tackle first. Take into consideration where you are in life and your current skill set. If becoming a professional hockey player is a goal that you have decided is attainable, that goal has a short shelf life and you should probably act on this in the short term. However, if there is no real urgency in terms of accomplishing any of the goals on your list, review the list and determine which one speaks to you and will bring you the greatest satisfaction once it becomes a reality. As my friend reminded me, *someday* is not a day of the week. Write down the short-range goals and actual target dates for completion. Consider the amount of time you have each day to commit to your plan based on your current lifestyle and responsibilities and be prepared to make some sacrifices.

Step 6: Create an Assist List

You need to decide who and what will help you on your journey to attain your chosen goal. Make a list of friends, family members, acquaintances, and experts who you can rely upon for emotional support, guidance, and knowledge. Also, write down what you might need in terms of more tangible items. It is tough to become a hockey player without ice skates or to run a race without running shoes! Consider, too, if you need classes, training, certification, etc., to follow a particular life course.

All of the other steps up until now help you shorten the list. There is one more step. I call these the W-H questions: Who? What? Where? Why? How? For each goal, answer the following questions:

1. Who do I need to know to reach my goal?
2. What do I need to know to reach my goal?
3. Where do I have to go to reach my goal?
4. Why am I trying to reach this goal?
5. How can I reach this goal?

You might have to think for a while before answering, and it is fine to take your time as you consider options and obstacles. I suggest taking one day to focus on a particular goal. Turn to the first page of your journal. Look at all the information you have written. From this point forward, everything should be written in sentences and paragraphs. Record your thoughts by asking and answering questions. Who do you need to know to reach this goal? What do you need to know to reach this goal? Where do you need to be to reach this goal? Write as much as you can. Take a substantial period of uninterrupted time to do so.

The most effective goal-setting tool I have used involves writing a plan and keeping a record of my progress. Writing things down helped organize and clarify my thoughts and strategies. Keeping a daily and weekly journal allowed me to track progress and provided perspective. It helped me see whether I was connecting the dots by attaining my short-term measurable objectives, which would in turn lead to the realization of my long-range goals. I would write both my successes and my failures in my journal. Periodically reviewing my journal gave me a thirty-thousand-foot view rather than looking at my goals through a keyhole. This broad, holistic viewpoint helped me see whether I was moving closer or further away from my goal. I could review the pattern of my actions in order to propagate efficient progress toward my goals.

Look at Those Goals Again!

Hopefully, I helped you map out a course for your upcoming journey, a journey that never truly ends. You should always be setting new goals for yourself and reevaluating your current ones.

Reevaluating your goals is crucial for several reasons: one, new opportunities can arise that you do not want to slip away; two, you can endure personal setbacks that may require you to redistribute your energies; and three, you will grow and change. Things that once were important may become less so and vice versa. All of these circumstances create the need to reevaluate your goals periodically.

Do you recall the section regarding luck, when I asked you to throw out any potential goals that depend on luck? Of course, I suggested doing this since you cannot plan to be lucky. Many people lose their shirts, their fortunes, their families, or worse, trying to gamble their way to their goals. On the other hand, if luck hands you a golden opportunity, you cannot be so wedded to a set of goals that you refuse to reexamine and reprioritize, thereby allowing an opportunity to pass.

Do you recall the story of Charles Goodyear, the American inventor? He found luck amidst a sea of adversity. In the town of New Haven, Connecticut, Charles Goodyear, at the age of 21, formed a partnership with his father in a hardware business. Unfortunately, the Goodyears encountered bad luck, culminating in the failure of their business. For many years, the younger Goodyear used his time to experiment with natural rubber, trying to find a way to alleviate brittleness when it became cold and stickiness when exposed to heat. His discoveries moved him to buy the patent rights to permeate sulfur into rubber from a rival inventor named Nathaniel Hayward. In 1893, Goodyear accidentally dropped a piece of sulfur-treated rubber onto a hot stove. When the rubber combined with the high temperature of the stove, the result was a natural rubber possessing the properties scientists were trying to discover. Just by luck, Goodyear's discovery unearthed a process called vulcanization, which, even today, is the basis of the rubber manufacturing industry.

Just as good fortune can open some doors, life's setbacks may temporarily close them, forcing you to reexamine your quest and map a new route to your destination.

Shakespeare's Hamlet asks, in his famous soliloquy, "For who would bear the whips and scorns of time?" Life has plenty of whips and scorns for us all.

How you confront life's challenges can be a defining moment. You have most likely heard stories of people, perhaps friends or relatives, who have accomplished unbelievable feats in the face of nearly unbearable adversity. Let me share one example with you.

There once was a woman who learned to speak much later in life than most, but she eventually mastered this skill in only one short month. Ten years later, she entered Radcliffe College, and she graduated with honors in 1904. Later, she served on the Massachusetts Commission for the Blind and traveled and lectured in more than eight countries, raising funds for the American Foundation for the Blind. As a pacifist and socialist, she traveled throughout Europe, visiting World War II veterans and lecturing on behalf of the physically handicapped. She wrote seven books and had a motion picture and a play written about her life. The reason she was unable to speak as a young child was due to being profoundly deaf. She was also completely blind. You may have heard of her: Helen Keller. As I said before, how we choose to manage life's tribulations can define our very being.

People like Helen Keller are heroic and inspiring, overcoming adversity most of us will never know. However, you have within you the ability to handle your own challenges and problems in a manner that can create defining moments in your life and the lives of those around you. Problems rarely disappear. If you continually avoid them, they will come back to haunt you sooner or later. Problems should be treated as obstacles that can be dealt with and worked through. The four words that are important in this statement are *dealt with* and *worked through*.

When you are progressing toward your goals and a problem arises, ask yourself: Can I do anything about this problem? If the answer is *no*, then ask: Since I have no control over this situation, what is the best way to deal with it? However, if the answer to the first question is *yes*, then ask yourself: What is the first step in solving this problem? By defining both the problem and the first step to overcoming it, you gain perspective on the situation immediately and perhaps even experience a sense of relief that comes from having a concrete plan. When you have formulated a plan to solve the problem, you may need to revisit and revise your goals. In doing so, you may actually discover a new pathway to your goal. As Shakespeare most elegantly wrote, "Sweet are the uses of adversity." Adverse conditions can create a better you.

A final reason to reevaluate your goals is your growth and development. Change is life's only constant. The wind and the weather, the passing of the day into the night and night into the day, the slipping of one season into the next—all sing a song of change, as do our brains, our bodies, and our beliefs. Your goals will change as you mature and broaden your perspective. Working in a disciplined way toward your goals will change you as a person. You will grow in ability and understanding.

As you change, so should your goals. Long-range goals may become short-term objectives as you near your destination. Goals can also shift in terms of importance. Resources that you once lacked may become available; conversely, resources you believed would be omnipresent may have vanished. In these situations, and in many others, restarting the process of goal setting can be like a sailor's sextant and compass, enabling you to ground yourself before charting a safe course forward.

Look at your journal and the timeline you created for each objective leading you to your ultimate goal. Every step is an accomplishment worthy of pause and a pat on the back. If others have helped you achieve one of the objectives along the way, now is the time to celebrate together and thank them. If you have achieved this goal via your own grit and wit, take some time for self-reward by doing something you like.

Step 7: Write a plan of action and record your progress

Do not expect your travels to progress at a pleasantly stable and steady pace. Just like the running back scampering toward the goal line, getting thumped and bumped around by those goliath linemen, you too will be knocked off course here and there in your journey to your personal end zone. Every day may not result in forward motion. You may take one step forward and two steps back from time to time. Nevertheless, by staying the course and keeping your eye on the prize, you will reach your destiny. Short-term goals and objectives provide landmarks you can more readily reach, unlike your ultimate goal, which may still exist in the land of implausibility. Since you will find yourself straying off course, either by your own volition or by unexpected cosmic forces (and I want to make it clear; you will be taken off course, not *may* be taken off course), and the pervading thought is, *I don't think I will ever reach my goal*, you will, in time, become quite adept at reframing. *I hit a bump in the road and will be back on track tomorrow* will be your mantra to staying true to your plan and the actions needed to reach your objectives.

Adopting the philosophy of "it is not a matter of if; it is a matter of *when"* is the best way to keep climbing the ladder to reach your goal. Indeed, an interesting phenomenon occurs when you refuse to give in. In your quest to become stronger, more capable, more adroit, and more successful, you need to be thrown off course from time to time. A goal that is too easy for you to attain does not contribute to your growth and development. A goal or objective that is effortless is merely a task on your to-do list that needs to be completed for that day. A goal that makes you stretch and strain through the process is the one that makes you grow and become a better person.

If you want to get physically stronger, you need to lift a weight to the point of failure when you are no longer able to lift it. If you are strong enough to lift a twenty-pound dumbbell for ten repetitions but the last two or three reps are a struggle, what is the amount of weight you should use to increase your strength and muscle mass? If you use a three-pound weight and lift it for ten repetitions without breaking a sweat, you will not increase your overall strength or muscle mass. It is relative. We all have to start somewhere on this continuum of skills as it applies to our goals.

As you navigate the goal-setting highway, you fully intend to grow and develop during the process, but you may not truly comprehend what you have gained in this quest. If you set a lofty goal but do not attain it, you may find that you grew more from the journey than by actually reaching your destination. This is the thesis of this book.

Remember in the introduction, when I talked about wanting to be a national champion but fell short of this goal five times in a row? Each year, going into the next competition with hope, I walked away with bronze medals. However, during the process, I gained the skill, knowledge, education, confidence, self-esteem, and passion for the work I do today. I truly believe that if I won the gold medal, I would not have the perspective that I have today: a perspective that the victory lies in the attempt, the courage, and the faith in believing that things will work out for the better. Goal setting is more than just getting something; it is becoming something better than you are today!

Two factors have a long-lasting impact on your life as you go about setting a goal. The first is that life conveniently provides you with ups and downs that require you to adjust and readjust, preventing you from becoming stagnant or languishing in the doldrums of a life devoid of aspirations. Second, while you may not have the skill to be able to reach the big goal just yet, you will continually grow as you reach smaller target goals and build the skills necessary to reach your ultimate goal.

Goals: A Journey or a Destination?

The journey to a goal is not a straight line. There are peaks and valleys, twists and turns awaiting you every step of the way. The following chart illustrates the progress toward a goal as it begins in the bottom left corner, eventually resting in the upper right corner of the graph, indicating the end of the goal and success!

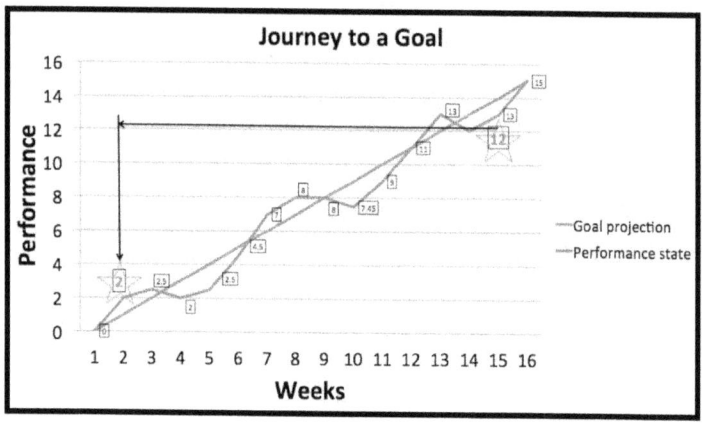

The line moves above and below the straight line (trend line), indicating the oscillating performances for each week. However, if you view the graph as a moving picture versus a snapshot over the course of the fourteen weeks, the behavior improves sixfold. Simply stated, this person's performance is six times better than it was at the onset. Even though the performance dipped below the goal line at times, to become six times better at something and to improve the behavior is quite an accomplishment. Therefore, no matter what your goal is, you will have good days, weeks, months, even years. If you stay the course, you will continually gain the skills necessary to reach the goal you set.

If you are setting lofty goals, some of them may initially be out of your reach and impossible to obtain with your current skill set. However, if you devise a realistic plan to accomplish your intermediate goals, eventually you will acquire the skills necessary to reach your final one.

Let us go back to the strength-training example. If your goal is to do fifty push-ups in a row, which is a lofty goal for most of us, you will need to build strength and endurance. This requires setting short-term goals and building on them over time. Your goals for the first week may be to complete a measly five push-ups, a virtual chasm from fifty, but likely a realistic objective. Soon five push-ups is no longer a challenge, so you move to your next rung on the ladder and work to do ten. Over time, you increase your output from fifteen to twenty, to twenty-five, then thirty, moving right along to forty, forty-five, and finally reaching fifty—goal reached!

Wow, how did you go from five to fifty? It was not a miracle or a magic trick, that is for sure. It was good old-fashion hard work. Throw in some time, a lot of energy, a dash of consistency, and a smidge of patience and persistence, mix it up, and you are churning out fifty push-ups … and the bragging rights to go along with reaching that goal. This example illustrates that you may not have the strength or skill to accomplish a goal today, but with time, energy, persistence, and a good plan, you can go from five to fifty!

CHAPTER 14

Focus: The Only Way to Set Your Life on Fire

One sleepless night, I found myself watching The Discovery Channel. The show featured a Shaolin master demonstrating his amazing skill of precision accuracy. I fully expected to be entertained by amazing martial arts feats showcasing jumping ability, outstanding power punches, and lightning fast kicks. However, I found myself riveted to the television by a performance that was completely unexpected. It was the Shaolin master's ability to fire a tiny pin through a 3mm-thick pane of glass! To prove that that the pin actually penetrated the glass, a blue balloon hung on the other side of the pane, ready to burst once the pin went through the windowpane.

Preparing for the demonstration, the master took deep breaths. His arms swung smoothly across his body as he focused intently on the target. Holding the pin in his hand, he then whipped his arm back, bent both knees, and unleashed the pin from his hand faster than the eye could follow. At that instant, the balloon burst. It really was a remarkable demonstration of skill and technique.

The narrator went on to explain that the way this is accomplished is through the Shaolin master's use of Qi (energy), an energy that comes from within a person's body. By focusing all the Qi or energy into one spot, the master transferred the tremendous energy from his entire body to his arm, and then to his fingertips, on to the needle, which pierced the pane and popped the balloon. I thought about this for days afterwards. The Shaolin master accomplished this by tapping into his natural energy source. Think about how this could translate into your own life if you utilized the power you could muster simply by focusing that energy with singular purpose.

Just as the focused energy of the Shaolin master was transferred to the needle, similarly, the sun's rays focus their energy to create tremendous heat. I remember summer days when I was a kid and a kitchen calendar replete with empty blocks: no appointments, no practices, not a whole lot of structure to my days. However, being typically curious and creative lads, my brother and I always managed to find ways to entertain ourselves. One day we discovered we could burn dry leaves with a magnifying lens. We would go out on sunny days around noon, when the sun was at its highest point, armed with our magnifying glass, and would slide into our alter egos as junior pyromaniacs. We realized we needed to hold the magnifying lens in just the right spot and at just the right angle to radiate enough to make a flame. Holding it too far away dissipated the sun's rays and did not provide the concentration of heat necessary to start a fire. Too close and the point of concentration was too small to disperse the heat to the rest of the leaf. We also discovered that if we moved the lens, the sun's rays did not have enough time to generate heat in that particular spot to start a fire, so it was crucial to maintain a steady hold on the lens.

The lessons we derived from our mischievous prank generalized nicely to other aspects of life. You see, it is not enough to focus on one thing at a time, but the focus needs to be directed in the right place, with the right amount of intensity, to accomplish anything. If you keep moving around, jumping from one project to the next, without ever giving it the right amount of time, thought, and energy, you may become frustrated and disenchanted to the point of abandoning your goal.

This lesson is exemplified by the actions of a man who continually demonstrated razor sharp focus. This focus saved his life more than one time. We know him best when he stepped on the moon on July 20, 1969. Once standing firmly on the surface of the moon, Neil Armstrong uttered those unforgettable words: "That's one small step for man, one giant leap for mankind." Armstrong's journey to be selected to be the man to first step on the lunar surface was a journey of practice, experience, and talent. However, most of all, it was focus. As a young boy, Armstrong fell in love with flight and aviation. His opportunity to fly came early in his life. He received his pilot's license before his driver's license. Later, Armstrong found himself flying fighter planes in the Korean War. During one mission, the enemy shot up his plane, destroying part of the wing. With a cool head and unyielding concentration, he quickly learned that if he maintained a certain speed, he could keep the plane in flight, but if it slowed under a certain speed, the plane would likely lose altitude and crash. He was able to pilot the damaged craft far enough and bail out safely, saving his life.

This would not be the only occasion in which he saved his life or the lives of those who flew with him.

Later, he became one of the most elite test pilots in the world. Proving he could take on more complicated flying machines as a naval aviator, he was given more and more difficult aircraft to test. One in particular was the X-15, which was part plane, part rocket. This aircraft zoomed to heights above the earth's atmosphere at six times the speed of sound. When the X-15 became weightless, Armstrong lost the ability to control the aircraft. Again, keeping a cool head, he waited until the plane bit into thicker air, allowing him to regain control of the instruments. The complexity of these machines needed a talent like Armstrong who possessed the ability to think quickly, rationally, and maintain that ultra-focus to test these machines under the most daunting circumstances. This included the Gemini 8 mission, which was designed to test the docking procedure of two spacecraft.

When entering NASA, Armstrong found himself training in the Lunar Landing Training Vehicle (LLTV), a training machine designed to allow astronauts to practice a lunar landing. During a practice flight, Armstrong lost control, and just seconds before the vehicle crashed, he ejected, parachuting safely to the ground. In the documentary *In the Shadow of the Moon*, Alan Bean relates a story where another astronaut says to him, "Did you hear that Neil bailed out of the LLTV today?"

Bean says, "No way!" To see if it was true, Bean returned to Armstrong and said, "I just heard the funniest story!"

Armstrong said, "What?"

"I heard that you bailed out of the LLTV an hour ago. I can't think of another person," Bean recalls, "let alone another astronaut, who would have just gone back to his office after ejecting a fraction of a second before getting killed."

This clearly exemplifies Armstrong's aptitude to focus on what was in front of him and not to be mired by past experiences, thereby ranking him among the most elite of the fighter pilots, test pilots, and astronauts, not to mention the first man to walk on the moon.

From the Shaolin's pin, to my magnifying lens, to Armstrong's walk on the moon, it takes a concentrated effort to incorporate the appropriate amount of speed, force, confidence, and skill to create the focus needed to succeed. Keeping all the distractions from your mind gives you the ability to accomplish more than you could if you were thinking of or trying to accomplish several things at once. Unwavering focus is essential to success, no matter what outcome you are pursuing. Think about one thing at a time and develop the focus of an astronaut.

CHAPTER 15

Self-Talk: The Best Way to Motivate Yourself to Do Anything!

Our problems are man-made. Therefore, they can be solved by man.
—John F. Kennedy

Last summer my family and I were visiting my brother and his newly acquired puppy. As pups do, he raced around for quite a while, playing with my boys. After about an hour, the dog sat down in the yard, stretched contentedly in the warm rays of the sun, taking in his surroundings. My six-year-old son piped up, "Daddy, what do you think he is thinking about?" As I searched for a pithy response to his question, I found myself in a quandary: *What is that dog thinking about?* Dogs do not speak English, French, or German. Even German Shepherds do not speak German. So, what do they think about? What do dogs say to themselves? Do they hear barking in their heads like we hear words when we think? Who knows? But I had to answer the young lad by admitting, "I have no idea what he is thinking."

As I continued to ponder, my son replied, "He is probably thinking about the trees and birds." His answer was as good as any I could offer. After that short exchange, I continued to puzzle over this question. As far as we know, animals do not use the same language as humans in the manner that we do. We have a complicated language system that uses letters that make up words, and these words are symbols of meaning and an avenue of communicating thoughts, ideas, concepts, and philosophies. However, this form of communication originates in the mind of the individual. It starts with thinking and that form of thinking is your internal dialogue, which is also known as self-talk.

Right now, you have the chatter of the words you are reading running through your mind. Even as you read these words, your mind may be wandering a bit and you might find yourself thinking about something else. In both instances, you were thinking and the words were front and center in your mind. Our thoughts control how what we feel about something influences how we behave, and thus how we respond to a situation. This, among other things, is what makes us different from a dog, a cat, or a horse. Animals' responses are largely a function of their genetic makeup and, therefore, they act in response to their environment. A dog does not say, "Maybe I should refrain from barking at that bird. I might wake up my master." No. The dog sees the bird, gets the urge, and barks. It is that simple.

Let me ask you something: Have you ever seen something and just "barked" out without thinking of the consequences? I am sure you have. We all have. We have both a genetic component to respond, such as when we pull our hands away from a hot surface, but also a learned one. We have the ability to formulate thoughts, evaluate the consequences, and make decisions. This separates humans from other members of the animal kingdom. However, if we do not pay attention to those thoughts racing through our heads, we become *responders* rather than *self-talkers*.

Have you ever heard the phrase, "Is the dog wagging its tail? Or is the tail wagging the dog?" I think this is the premise of our self-talk. We can control our self-talk from within, much like the dog wagging its tail. When external factors control what we say to ourselves, the tail is wagging the dog. Either way, what you say to yourself or what someone says to you influences you. The words in your mind reverberate. It is important to know how the words got there, who is saying them, and what is being said. We talk to ourselves all the time both consciously and unconsciously. "As you think so you shall be" is an ancient phrase that rings true even to this day.

This internal dialogue can create a cacophony of feelings, depending on what you say, how you say it, and how you interpret these words. Did you ever do something and then think, *Gee, that was stupid. I can't believe I did that!*? This is an example of having a conversation with yourself. Choosing the words that move from one side of your brain to the other not only affects your feelings and behaviors, but can also impact your sense of worth. In his book *Mental Training for Peak Performance*, Dr. Steven Ungerleider says, "Self-talk and self-affirmations become great emotional strengths when they enhance self-esteem and self-worth. It works to great advantage when this self-improvement leads to a terrific performance."

If you are watching a sporting event, you can often guess what athletes are saying to themselves just by their facial expressions. You might even see them mouthing the words or saying them aloud, even though no one is within earshot. That is self-talk. You can witness the joy and excitement in their faces as they clench their fists and silently say "Yes!" after a great play. No words, just their lips moving. They are not talking to anyone, only themselves, either applauding their performances or condemning it. Self-talk is a very powerful tool.

Self-talk is the rudder that keeps you moving in the right direction. If you find yourself wavering, you can regain your footing simply by employing self-talk. It can be the pep talk you need in times of despair or apathy. People who are depressed project despondency in their internal discourse; people who are happy espouse joy and optimism in their self-contained chats. At a basic level, it is pretty simple.

I have a friend who, regardless of the scenario, is always conjuring up the worst possible outcome in her head. She proclaims, "Oh, this is going to be terrible," prior to any event. (Remember the half-empty concept I talked about earlier in this book? If you want to know what it takes to be a half-empty person, here's how you do it!) How do you think my friend feels when she says this kind of thing? Bad feelings rush through her blood and she responds in kind. She is shrouded in gloom and doom. Her self-talk barrages her with erroneous thoughts and feelings as she tells herself something will undoubtedly go wrong—and guess what? It *does* go wrong. If you sow the seeds of negativity, you reap misery. Unfortunately, she lets her self-talk morph into actual conversation with others, which can make for a melancholy gathering.

I have another friend who, no matter what happens, says, "Don't worry about it. Everything will work out. It will just take a little time." What feelings are racing through his system? Yes, you guessed it. He has the feeling of hope, possibility, and control. His sense of well-being is intact, and realizing he has options and control makes his life more pleasant. He also recognizes that over time, most situations can improve, which generates a feeling of hopefulness. Of course, some things are not that simple and things may not get better. Nevertheless, while you are going through those bad times, it is a hell of a lot easier to face misfortune if you are able to convince yourself that things will work out in some fashion. So which of my friends do you think is more pleasant to be around on a daily basis? Who do you think would be a better leader? Unequivocally, the latter is the person with whom you want to associate. So what is the difference?

You can set yourself up for success by using positive self-talk, and you alone get to pick the message. You are in complete control of what you say to yourself. If the words of others echo in your head, do not feel compelled to incorporate them into your internal dialog. Ultimately, you choose what you say to yourself and the associated feelings. This is the power of self-talk.

Many of us incorporate the same self-talk on a daily basis. This habit can be a bad thing if you employ phrases that cause frustration rather than fervor. If your self-talk is replete with positive statements and motivation, it can help you stay in the present and totally focused on a task. Using such self-talk in a consistent manner will produce positive action and make your actions automatic, consequently heightening your intuition. A sense of mindfulness will become the norm. Things around you will seem more obvious as your internal dialogue becomes more positive.

With self-talk to motivate you and fill you with the desire to be successful, still another tool takes you to that next level once you master it. It is the use of visualization and mental imagery.

CHAPTER 16

Vision: Seeing to Believing to Creating

Look around you. Take notice of the things you see that are man-made. Your desk, the carpet, a phone, or the chair in which you are sitting were all fabricated. However, before they were constructed, they were merely a vision conjured up in someone's mind. This person may have had a very specific structure, style, and color in mind before the materials were collected. How about the house or apartment in which you live or the bridge you drive over every day? Those, too, were all products of someone's imagination and vision at one point.

The best athletes, business professionals, and leaders have the capacity to create a clear picture of what lies ahead. The Olympic athlete can envision running all out, crossing the finish line, and then feeling the heavy gold around her neck as she stands to listen to her country's national anthem. The business professional foresees handshakes and signatures after a marvelous sales presentation. The mission leader visualizes the group completing their project safely and successfully. A common characteristic among successful people is the ability to create a clear vision of what they want to accomplish. Whether leading yourself or others, a clear mental picture must first be established in your mind. Remember the chair that is built first in the mind of the builder before any materials are purchased? So, how do you go about creating that vision for your future?

There are several mental aspects to learning how to build your vision. The first is self-talk, which I described earlier. More specifically, it is the words you use that facilitate this process and impact how you view the future. You can hear it in people's language if a vision is present or not.

I have a friend whom I consider to be an effective leader. Not only is she able to help me see her vision of what she is trying to accomplish, but she is able to communicate with unabashed confidence and optimism. She says things like, "Did you ever imagine …?" or, "Try to look at it this way." Or she will offer a personal perspective: "The way I see it is …" Do you see the kinds of words she uses to communicate her vision? She uses sight words such as *imagine*, *see*, and *look* that describe her ideas and provide me with a clearer image of what she is thinking. She is the production manager of her own mental film company, a cinema of the mind. As she explains what she wants to accomplish, I am on set, viewing the production of the movie scene that exists only in her thoughts. I can actually feel what she is saying and the passion behind her words. Her vivid description makes her ideas come alive as I walk with her down the path to living the vision she is producing.

Most of us can create an image of some sort in our mind or on paper, but seeing that vision become a reality requires an emotional investment. Great leaders, like my friend, use mental imagery on a daily basis. Mental imagery helps you tap into all your senses and engulfs you in the moment of the experience before the experience even happens. It is the tapestry of the foundation necessary to turn dreams into your realities.

Managing your vision also takes a deep sense of purpose and belief that makes your vision become reality. Highly skilled leaders are able to communicate their vision not just to others, but also to themselves, with an unshakable belief in what they want for themselves and others. They talk beyond current reality, which creates inspiration, perspiration, and passion for a new reality. The leader makes the impossible possible for themselves, their team, and for the world. This sharable vision creates inspiration and motivation for all, and if shared with enough people, it creates a tipping point where real change happens. A clear vision creates the mission for you to follow. Having a clear vision and mission is essential to drafting a strategy to create a different reality.

CHAPTER 17

Mental Rehearsal: Making Your Dreams a Reality

Helen Keller stated, "The most pathetic person in the world is someone who has sight but no vision."

Friedrich Nietzsche declared, "The visionary lies to himself, the liar only to others."

William Blake avowed, "If the doors of perception were cleansed, everything would appear to man as it is—infinite."

Victor Hugo affirmed, "Nothing is more imminent than the impossible ... what we must always foresee is the unforeseen."

Lastly, from the great football coach Tony Dungy, "The first step toward creating an improved future is developing the ability to envision it. VISION will ignite the fire of passion that fuels our commitment to do WHATEVER IT TAKES to achieve excellence. Only VISION allows us to transform dreams of greatness into the reality of achievement through human action. VISION has no boundaries and knows no limits. Our VISION is what we become in life."

Many people wander through life only responding to the hand they have been dealt rather than doing the dealing. This is why many people never really get what they deserve. However, I've observed that many people do not really *know* what they want. As I mentioned earlier, our fast-paced society leaves little time for us to really think about what we want. People typically manage to satisfy their basic needs, but never really take the time to clearly define what they actually want in life. Having a clear vision of the future is the first step in realizing your destiny.

Some time ago, an associate and I were talking about the idea of him knowing what he wanted and being able to envision that thought as a reality. I mentioned that often, people's ideas are haphazardly constructed and unorganized. This is perfectly normal and innocuous if you do not intend to achieve what it was you were thinking about; however, this is not tolerable if you intend to make this thought/wish/dream a reality. Emerson said, "Good thoughts are no better than good dreams, unless they be executed!"

Without focus, you may become frustrated and abandon the idea and the ultimate vision you once had. It is imperative to have a vision that is clearly constructed, reflected upon intensely, and visualized, and then telling yourself it *will* happen. Clearly seeing yourself winning the race, making the big sale, being financially independent, taking your company public, being fifty pounds lighter, meeting the person of your dreams, or having a family, are all things people wish for. Most never define in their minds what this will actually look and feel like.

So, now that we have identified the problem, what actions need to be taken to solve it? After all, I just proposed that it is perfectly normal to have disorganized thoughts. Remember, you are not a tree immobilized by your deep-seated roots; you have the ability to do something and take action. When a thought enters your mind, it is often fleeting. It slips into your consciousness and most times leaves just as quickly as it arrived. This is important to understand, because you need your dreams to stay around long enough to become ingrained in your subconscious. Your subconscious needs the opportunity to take over and turn your dream that could have been dismissed as a flight of fancy into reality.

Consider this: When you toss a ball to an American child, his automatic response is to catch it with his hands. His subconscious knows the predominant American sports are baseball and football, both of which emphasize the use of the hands over the feet. Conversely, when a European child sees a ball coming to him, his subconscious response is to use his body to control the ball and to bring it to his feet, because the predominant sport in his culture is soccer. In this case, the two children's subconscious responds in the same exact way, but with different manifested responses.

Were you visualizing this scene as I described the differences between these two children? Perhaps you had a picture in your mind of a child, maybe wearing blue jeans and a green shirt, or maybe wearing green shorts and a blue shirt. Maybe you pictured your own child. Maybe your visualization was taking place indoors, or perhaps it was outdoors on a sunny day. Initially you saw the child catching the ball in his hands, but when an alternate idea was introduced, you were able to incorporate that into a brand new visualization. By activating your subconscious, you turn on your consciousness to assist you to establish clear pictures, even ones you previously had not considered. It is kind of like the light at the end of the tunnel: you need to give your subconscious a vision to where it needs to take you. So, why am I emphasizing the subconscious so much? *Because the subconscious has the ability to influence and even trick and redirect your conscious self if necessary.*

How do we maximize the influence of the subconscious over the conscious? It is easier than you might think. Consider the very common goal of weight loss. First, you must define your goal, perhaps losing twenty pounds. You then need to visualize how you would look twenty pounds lighter. You can even close your eyes to make your vision clearer. Before long, you will start to have a clearer picture of yourself when you reach the goal. Now you need to idealize your vision. Imagine looking good on the beach, dressing up for a party, buying new "skinny" clothes. You need to associate a variety of positive aspects with your goal in order to see them in more depth and detail.

For example, when you are imagining yourself looking good on the beach, think about how the sun might feel on your skin, or the relaxed feeling you get while listening to the waves, or how good that strawberry daiquiri will taste. What happens is, by associating weight loss with these positive feelings, your subconscious will now begin to *always* associate weight loss with the warmth of the sun on your skin, or crashing waves, or a strawberry daiquiri. Then, when you are doing something completely unrelated, such as washing dishes (associated with crashing waves), your subconscious reminds your conscious self of your goal.

Imagine that you are in the park walking your dog and the sun peeks out from behind the clouds. It warms your face. Your subconscious will then remind your conscious self of your goal of losing twenty pounds and, as a result, you will be inspired to finish the walk with your dog at a faster pace in order to burn some additional calories. As you see, the sun on your face does not directly cause you to lose weight, but the sun on your face triggers the scene of you on the beach in your new svelte body and propels you toward your goal of losing weight.

The technical term to what I just described is what psychologists call the *visual motor behavior rehearsal (VMBR)*. Physiologically, what happens is that your body is unable to distinguish between what is real and what you imagine; therefore, if your subconscious communicates with your body, your body is unable to determine if the message is coming from your conscious self or your subconscious. When you repeat an action often enough, it becomes ingrained into your nervous system. This process has even been demonstrated in controlled laboratory experiments. One experiment has track and field athletes connected to biofeedback equipment. They are then instructed to visualize themselves competing. Scientists discovered an interesting thing: the same muscles fired in the same sequence when they were running the event in their mind as when they were running it on the track.

The message is clear: do not underestimate the power of a vision.

CHAPTER 18

Simulation: Planning, Practice, Patience Makes Perfect

In a world of instant communication including text messages and tweets, planning, practice, and patience are becoming a lost art. Does the following scene sound familiar? You text your friend: Hey, do you want to meet for pizza? You wait ... five seconds ... ten seconds ... You are becoming annoyed. You put your phone down and take a deep breath. A minute passes, then two. You pick up your phone to see if maybe you missed the *ding* of your friend's response. You debate, *Maybe I sent it to the wrong person ... should I re-text? Maybe he's ignoring me.* Five minutes pass. You decide to grab a burger on your way home and post something on Facebook to make your (former) friend feel guilty.

The mindset of expecting immediate responses is a potential problem when we are seeking results that may need time to mature. Many projects and plans need time to develop. They require planning, work, practice, and patience to come to fruition. Great things rarely happen overnight.

It takes years to develop the skills to become an Olympian, to earn a Ph.D., to become a master plumber, or a physician. Obviously, you do not just wake up one day, look in the mirror, and say, "I guess today I will report to my local hospital and perform heart surgery." (However, I must tell you, if you did show up at your local hospital one day proclaiming you were there to perform heart surgery on someone, they would most likely call security and happily escort you to a different hospital, with different kinds of doctors who would be examining your head!)

If you plan to become a doctor, you need to take into account the many years of education, training, hard work, dedication, sacrifices, and commitment you must be prepared to make: four years of pre-med courses before qualifying for admittance to four more years of medical school; an intense year of internship; and two years as a resident doctor, all in order to successfully pass the medical boards and be dubbed a bona fide medical doctor. Ten years later, you are finally able to work as a doctor, and this doesn't include the extra training it takes to become a specialist.

That is a bit longer than the text message you were waiting for from your friend, right? An ambitious undertaking of any sort requires patience, planning, practice, hard work, and, of course, time. It is this amalgamation of prolonged experiences that molds a person into becoming a success. It is a process that cannot be rushed.

Consider those people who continually demonstrate the commitment and mental toughness necessary to work in the Special Operations branch of the United States military. The incredible feats of courage they perform to protect our nation are remarkable on so many levels. The U.S. Navy SEALs is one such unit that exemplifies planning, practice, and patience.

An article in *Newsweek's* 2014 July/August special edition featured an array of Special Operations forces. The issue, titled *Special Ops: Inside the Secret World of America's Elite Warriors*, features an article about SEAL Team 6, considered the most elite of all the SEAL teams. While reading this article, I was astonished to learn what these men go through to attain the level of skill needed to perform their jobs.

The article begins, "The road to SEAL Team 6 is paved with wave torture, hypothermic conditions, and a lot of swimming with your hands behind your back." The journey starts in Navy boot camp and consists of eight weeks of relentless training. After boot camp, and if they meet the Navy SEAL requirements, candidates move on to the indoctrination and pre-training phase, which is five to nine weeks long. This is where "Candidates must be able to swim one thousand yards with fins in less than twenty minutes; perform at least seventy push-ups in two minutes; do at least ten pull-ups in two minutes; do at least sixty curl-ups in two minutes; and run four miles wearing boots and pants in less than thirty-one minutes," according to the article.

Now, remember, this is just the pre-training. Completing pre-training qualifies them for an introduction to Basic Underwater Demolition or BUD/s, which lasts three weeks. The following seven weeks include three phases. Phase 1 (basic conditioning) includes "Hell Week," which is five and a half days of training in which candidates are permitted to sleep a total of only four hours and participate in over twenty hours of physical training a day, which includes running more than two hundred miles over the course of the week. Phase 2 includes combat diving for seven more weeks, where they learn how to become combat swimmers. There is also open diving, scuba diving, and other types of advanced diving techniques. Phase 3 of training is Land Warfare Training. This is seven weeks involving training in weapons, demolition, land navigation, patrolling, rappelling, and marksmanship. Twenty-six more weeks include SEAL Qualification Training, including tactical air operations, close-quarters combat, medical skills, cold weather survival, static line parachuting, free-fall parachuting, and Survival, Evasion, Resistance, and Escape (SERE)."

Successfully passing all the training requirements and becoming a Navy SEAL is without question one of the most challenging ventures anyone could put himself through. Beyond this elite fraternity is an even more highly trained and skilled group considered the elite of the elite: SEAL Team 6. The article goes on to say, "Before consideration for SEAL Team 6, a candidate needs at least five years of field experience as a Navy SEAL. Team 6 members are selected from the most elite of the approximately two thousand five hundred existing SEALs and are interviewed by a panel of Team 6 operators and trainers in order to be invited to the selection team, known as the Green Team. The selection process involves between six and eight months of training and evaluation. Less than fifty percent make the cut." It is believed that out of the two thousand five hundred Navy SEALs, only two hundred to three hundred are SEAL Team 6 members. These men are trained in counterterrorism, counterinsurgency, sabotage, and assassination.

To be the best of the best, it takes an unwavering commitment to your goal, a good amount of time, and a lot of energy. The real trick with the men in the Special Forces is that they never give up. They just keep coming. Becoming really good at your craft means that you should never give up. Devoting consistent practice, day in and day out, will help you stay the course. No matter what gets in your way, you will be able to keep the faith that you will triumph. At times you might not feel you are making progress, but keeping your faith in the process and having the patience to let things unfold will help you get past those difficult times. Always believe that things will get better. Take it one day at a time. Keep the task in front of you and with you. I heard someone say, "Walk with the task at hand and it will walk with you." Having that focus will direct your mind to look for the kernels of hope that you might need when things seem bleak.

Whether you choose to pursue a career as a physician, devote your life to the safety and well-being of your country, or focus on becoming the best doggone carpenter in the county, devise a plan of patience and practice to foster your skills and reach your chosen target.

CHAPTER 19

Living in the Zone

Learn from the past, set vivid, detailed goals for the future, and live in the only moment of time over which you have any control: now.
—Denis Waitley

On February 15, 2006, Jim Johnson, a basketball coach at Greece Athena High School, called on student Jason McElwain to play the last four minutes of the team's final game of the season. Did the coach put Jason in because he was the go-to guy in tight situations? Actually, the Greece Athena basketball team had a comfortable double-digit lead with four minutes to go. Did the coach use Jason because he was the best defensive player and wanted to ensure the win? Probably not, since Jason had seen no playing time prior to this game. This was a purposeful decision made by Coach Johnson to send Jason into the game.

    Jason entered the game, gathered in a pass from his teammate, and attempted a three-point shot. He missed it wide. Receiving the ball for the second time, Jason missed the easy layup. Then lightning struck. Jason exploded by making six three-pointers and then a two-point shot before the buzzer sounded, ending the game. As the buzzer sounded, pandemonium erupted and the crowd went crazy, acknowledging Jason's twenty points in four minutes. Spectators and players alike stormed the court, celebrating the team's victory and congratulating Jason for his unbelievable play. Jason's amazing performance resulted in an impressive thirty-five-point victory for Greece Athena, with the final score showing Greece Athena seventy-nine, Spencerport forty-three.

In a post-game interview, a commentator remarked to Jason, "You just caught fire."

Jason responded, "Just caught fire? I was hot as a pistol!"

His performance made the local news that night and the national news soon after. Jason became a modern day celebrity. Various sports teams began to invite him to visit them. He visited the Florida men's basketball team the year they went on to win the National Championship. Later in the year, Jason was invited to spend some time with Indianapolis Colts quarterback Peyton Manning at the Colts' training camp. That year, Indianapolis won the Super Bowl. In 2007, the San Antonio Spurs basketball team won the NBA championship after Jason spent time with the team. He met President George W. Bush, who said, "… our country was captivated by your amazing story on the basketball court. I think it is a story of Coach Johnson's willingness to give a person a chance. It is a story of Dave and Debbie's deep love for their son, and it is a story of a young man who found his touch on the basketball court, which, in turn, touched the hearts of citizens all across the country."

At this point, you might be thinking that while Jason's four minutes of play was certainly impressive, the sports world is replete with truly incredible performances from high school, college, and professional players nearly every day. So what is the big deal about hitting some shots in a high school's team season finale against a pedestrian opponent? Was it really worthy of a visit with the president of the United States of America? Hundreds of great games and great performances occur across the country every day. Why is this kid, who was not even a player on the team, being invited to hang out with elite athletes? Face it; it is really exciting to score twenty points in a short period, but it does not typically catapult someone to celebrity status, right? So, why did Jason's performance spawn such a remarkable cascading magnetism and gravity toward this young man? What makes him so special?

Clearly, Jason was not the go-to guy to secure a win for the team. He was not the best defensive player on the team either. Jason was put in the game so that he could earn a jersey and sit for the team picture at the end of the season. In fact, Jason was not even a player on the team. Jason was the team manager. Jason McElwain has high functioning autism. Greece Athena's high school basketball team manager, a young man with a developmental disability, captivated an entire country in four minutes and everyone wanted to share in this celebration of spirit. From professional football to basketball players to the president of the United States, Jason touched the hearts of so many just by being in the moment, a moment that lasted only four minutes. His coach summed it up best when he was asked in an interview, "Is there something almost mystical about him that we don't realize?" The coach responded, "I think there is. I tell people in my speeches that it is the magic of J-Mac. I think the greatest thing in life is hope.

And I think this story is giving a lot of people hope. And another thing is, never give up on your dreams. We all have potential to do something really good in our lives, and that is a great lesson from the story and the game."

There is a lot to be learned from J-Mac. For one, there is magic in all of us. We all can hope more, dream more, and certainly, just like J-Mac, see vast potential and possibilities that are deep within us. This is the true inspiration shaped by a memorable four minutes. They were four minutes of intense focus and concentration that found J-Mac living in the moment, playing in the *zone*. Playing and living in the zone is where true happiness resides—being in that place where the past meets the future, where you are "in the moment" and "hotter than a pistol," as J-Mac put it, where everything seems to click. Performances and experiences become automatic when you get into what athletes often refer to as *being in the zone*, or what psychologist Mihaly Csikszentmihalyi calls *flow*.

In their book *Flow in Sports: The keys to optimal experiences and performances*, psychologists Susan A. Jackson and Mihaly Csikszentmihalyi talk about the concept of immersion in the present: "When all of the conditions for flow are present—clear goals, a steady stream of feedback, a matching of challenges and skills—concentration becomes more intense. Yet, paradoxically, it also seems more spontaneous. In other words, while attention is sharp and focused, it needs no effort to keep it so."

J-Mac's simple joy of playing in the game for a short time resulted in him finding the zone and experiencing a flow that produced twenty points of greatness.

Once you find yourself in the zone and experiencing flow, you, too, will find the task at hand unfolding before you. Doctors Jackson and Csikszentmihalyi go on to say, "The fact that concentration happens more effortlessly in flow is one of the reasons it is such an enjoyable state to be in. Staying focused on what you are doing ceases to be a struggle or a strain, and this allows complete involvement, which is a very satisfying state to experience."

This concept is reinforced for me as I recall attending a national judo training camp in Colorado Springs, Colorado, many years ago. I spent most of my summer training twice a day with the nation's best players and coaches, and the paces we were put through were the most challenging I had faced since I began practicing judo. The top instructor held a seventh-degree black belt and guided our advanced training that summer. A pioneer in American judo and martial arts, Phil Porter was one of the great coaches of the day.

During our three-hour training sessions, Porter would intersperse his philosophies of commitment, mindfulness, attitude, perspective, and life throughout our workouts while he punished us with exercise, drills, and hundreds of repetitions. Porter, a West Point graduate, served twenty-five years in the U.S. Army and Air Force. He eventually retired as a major in 1967. Porter's intelligence was obvious, his charisma contagious, and his leadership legendary. He demanded excellence and unwavering commitment from all of the students. He commanded that we focus every session on the tasks and drills he introduced. In one of our many long grueling sessions, he showed a millisecond of mercy, or at least that is how it appeared, when he stopped our training and began to speak to us in a serious, passionate tone.

He said, "During these intensive training sessions, you will have moments of doubt and despair in which you will think you cannot go on."

He then said something that I have never forgotten: "When these moments arrive, you must live where the *past meets the future*."

Porter proclaimed, "This is where champions live. Champions live in the *nick of time*. So, practice, strive, and fight in the moment. That is the only place you are now, and the only place you will be, where the past meets the future."

I was sixteen years old at the time he said those words, and I do not believe I will ever forget them. I have played that decree hundreds of thousands of times since in my mind. This is the only place we can be at any moment in time. Powerful! Being in the zone means you exist in this moment and this moment only, and not worrying about the past or the future. The past is over and the future is coming, so why think about either of them? We cannot let our performances be affected by these unknowns, neither of which we can do anything about. It is only the present moment that makes our happiness real. So, whether it is J-Mac or Jordan on the court, a lawyer in the courtroom, or you, finding the zone of optimal performance and happiness comes from within.

Conclusion

Honest and sincere personal development leads to true leadership: first, to lead yourself to where you want to go and be; and second, to lead others. Only then can you truly lead with confidence and competence. As you have discovered, the primary focus of this book is finding out what is actually hindering you from moving triumphantly toward your goals. Once you are aware of what is stopping you, the second part helps you build the solid foundation necessary to stand firm in order to reach your aspirations. Once you establish an unwavering basis, you then embark on seven steps to make your dreams a reality. So … go make your dreams a reality!

Afterword

Giving Back to Others

Leaders can let you fail and yet not let you be a failure.
–Stanley McChrystal, retired U.S. Army four-star general

As I mentioned in the introduction of this book, I believe that no skill is worth acquiring unless it can be transferred to helping others. I also think it is most fitting to close with this premise. However, there is a caveat to offering your skills to others to help them. I am not talking about enabling others, but, in fact, assisting others in finding their own abilities, talents, and passions. To do this, it takes courage and restraint to encourage, teach, and be there for our fellow men and women to help them learn the skills necessary to reach their own level of greatness. To return the favor to others is our greatest gift.

I would like to end this book with a story I heard many years ago that I believe exemplifies this notion of struggle and giving back. The story is titled *The Boy and the Butterfly*, and it goes like this:

Coming home from school one day, a young boy noticed a caterpillar on the branch of a tall tree next to his home. Each day he would stop and watch this caterpillar on the tree, but this day something was different. On this day, the boy noticed the creature hanging from the branch with silky webbing beginning to form around its body. After a few days, the cocoon totally encased the caterpillar, which hung gingerly from the tree. Day after day, the boy would stop and stare at the cocoon. He wondered what the little bug was doing in there. Was he sleeping? Then, on the hottest day of the year, he stopped, as he usually did, to visit the cocooned critter, only to notice for the first time a little movement. Wrapped tightly, the creature seemed to struggle as a tiny opening in the cocoon emerged. For the boy, the feeling of fascination felt juxtaposed with one of frustration for his friend and he felt a stir to help the animal escape its surly bonds. He raced home to retrieve a small sharp tool and carefully clipped the cocoon just enough to help the butterfly escape from the cocoon. The butterfly dropped onto a few brown dry leaves. Lying motionless, its body was moist and swollen, showing remnants of tiny shriveled wings. The boy was visibly distressed when it was unable to fly. He ran home to his mother to see if she could help. His face covered in tears, he desperately explained what he had done. His mother responded to her young son in her gentle motherly voice, saying, "My dear boy, the butterfly did not need your help to escape. Nature needs it to struggle." She explained that the butterfly's struggle to push its way through the tiny opening of the cocoon pushes the fluid out of its body and into its wings. This last action gives the butterfly the ability to fly free with the others. Without the struggle, the butterfly would never, ever fly.

We all have good intentions to help others, as you can see from this story. I think the real art in helping is not so much what we do, but the manner in which we go about doing it. As your own struggles have made you stronger and more capable, you must remember that giving back to those around you does not mean saving them to escape their challenges, but encouraging them to fight harder so that they, too, can become stronger and more capable.

As this book suggests over and over again, the quest for success and leadership always originates from hard work, determination, clear visions, total commitment, belief, and faith. We can all make a difference, and that difference starts with you!

About the Author

David Loshelder has a bachelor's degree from Pennsylvania State University and a master's degree from Duquesne University. He is the author of *Protect Yourself: Top 10 Lifesaving Self-Defense Techniques*. He lives with his wife and three sons in Pittsburgh, Pennsylvania. He also lectures to corporations, associations, and universities on personal achievement and leadership. He invites readers to email him at *Dave@takecareofnumberone.com*.

Bibliography

Air and Space Smithsonian. (n.d.). *Armstrong's Close Call*. Retrieved June 30, 2016, from www.AirSpace.com: http://www.airspacemag.com/videos/armstrongs-close-call/?no-ist

Association, U. S. (2014, January 10). *United States Martial Arts Association*. Retrieved January 25, 2016, from Phil Porter: http://wwmaa.org/phil-porter/

AZIZ. (2013, June 11). *On Prism*. Retrieved from azizonomics: http://azizonomics.com/2013/06/11/on-prism/

Baker, T. (2014, July/August). Navy SEALs. *Special Ops (1)*, *1*, 67-70. New York, New York, United States of America: Media Lab Publishing.

Bates, B. N. All in the Family. (D. Seeds, Ed.) *Smart Business, Insight Advice Strategy Special Edition*, *Special Edition*, 5-7.

Chicken Soup for the Soul Publishing, LLC. (2016). *Chickensoup for the Soul*. Retrieved September 17, 2015, from http://www.chickensoup.com/about/facts-and-figures

Collins, J. (2001). *Good To Great*. New York, New York: HarperCollins Publishers.

Collins, J., & Hansen, M. T. (2011). *Great by Choice*. New York, New York, USA: HarperCollins Publishers.

Connelly, M. (2014). *Change Management Coach*. Retrieved November 22, 2014, from Change Management Coach: http://www.change-management-coach.com/force-field-analysis.html

Csikszentmihalyi, M. (1990). *Flow: the psychology of optimal experience*. New York, New York, USA: Harper Perennial Modern Classics.

Csikszentmihalyi, M., & Jackson, S. A. (1999). *Flow In Sports: The Keys to Optimal Experiences and Performances.* United States of America: Human Kinetics.

Eklund, R. C., & Tenenbaum, G. (Eds.). (2014). Attention Training. *Encyclopedia of Sport and Exercise Psychology*, 45.

Gallwey, T. (1997). *The Inner Game of Tennis.* New York, New York: Random House.

Gill, C. (2015, January 1). *www.news.psu.edu.* Retrieved February 2, 2015, from Zombie ant fungi 'know' brains of their hosts: www.news.psu.edu

Godin, S. (2007). *the dip.* New York, New York: Penguin Group.

Greene, R. (2012). *Mastery.* New York, New York: Penguin Books.

Heller, M. (2012). *The DASH DIET Weight Loss Solution* (Vol. First Edition). New York, New York, United States: Grand Central Publishing.

Liggett, T. W. (1997). *The Inner Game of Tennis.* New York, New York: Random House.

M. Force Field Analysis. (n.d.). Retrieved February 22, 2016, from http://www.train4creativity.eu: http://www.train4creativity.eu/dat/77F14335/file.pdf

Merriam-Webster Dictionary. (1828). *Merriam-Webster.* Retrieved from http://www.merriam-webster.com: http://www.merriam-webster.com/dictionary/prism

Orlick. (2015, January 23). *Wikipedia.* Retrieved January 30, 2015, from Wikipedia: http://en.wikipedia.org/wiki/Circumstellar_habitable_zone

Orlick, T. (2000). *In Pursuit of Excellence*. United States of America : Human Kinetics .

Ormrod, J. *Human Learning*. New Jersey, United States: Merrill Prentice Publishers.

Pink, D. H. (2009). *Drive: The Surprising Truth About What Motivates Us*. New York, New York: Penguin Group.

Sington, D. (Director). (2008). *In The Shadow Of The Moon* [Motion Picture].

Smithsonian, Airs and Space. (n.d.). *Armstrong's Close Call*. Retrieved July 1, 2016, from www.airspacemag.com: http://www.airspacemag.com/videos/armstrongs-close-call/?no-ist

Starbucks, Inc. (2016). *www.startbucks.com*. Retrieved from investor.starbucks.com: http://investor.starbucks.com/phoenix.zhtml?c=99518&p=irol-newsArticle&ID=2131218

Swindoll, C. (. (n.d.). *Attitude by Charles Swindoll*. Retrieved December 27, 2014, from http://faculty.kutztown.edu/friehauf/attitude.html

TheMonartSpa. (2011, September 23). *Needle through glass.m4v*. Retrieved October 22, 2015, from www.youtube.com: https://youtu.be/Tn61Y99ON1U

Ungerleider, S. (1996). *Mental Training for Peak Performance*. Emmaus, Pennsylvania: Rodale Press, Inc.

What Are Black Holes And How Do They Die? (2014, January 21). Retrieved from penny4nasa.org: http://www.penny4nasa.org/2014/01/21/what-are-black-holes-and-how-do-they-die/

Wikipedia Foundation, Inc. (2014, December 20). Retrieved January 5, 2015, from http://www.beesmatter.ca/plant-reproduction-and-the-role-of-honey-bees/

Wikipedia Foundation, Inc. (2014, December 20). *Wikipedia*. Retrieved January 5, 2015, from Wikipedia: http://en.wikipedia.org/wiki/Learned_helplessness

Wikipedia Foundation, Inc. (2014, December 20). *Wikipedia*. Retrieved January 5, 2015, from Wikipedia: https://www.yahoo.com/finance/news/why-retired-navy-seal-commander-133500237.html

Wikipedia. (2016, April 23). *Jason McElwain*. Retrieved from Wikipedia Foundation, Inc. : https://en.wikipedia.org/wiki/Jason_McElwain

Youtube. (2012, May 15). *Famous Failures*. Retrieved December 22, 2015, from Youtube: https://www.youtube.com/watch?v=zLYECIjmnQs

Zaalesne, M. J. (2007). *Microtrends, The Small Forces Behind Tomorrow's Big Changes.* New York, New York , United States of America : Hachette Book Group USA.

Zigler, Z. (1988). Goals - Set goals...and reach them! *Goals - Set goals...and reach them!* Wheeling, IL, United States of America: Nightingale-Conant

Citations

Figure 1 (Force Field Analysis): Abstract figure pushing center block, Copyright Artenot © 123RF.com

Figure 3 Ten Commandments, Copyright Moises, 123rf.com

Index

A

adrenal gland 33, 34, 35
adrenaline 34, 35
Air Force 181
American Foundation for the Blind 141
arms race 57
Armstrong, Neil 151
astronauts 7, 111, 152, 153
astronomers 50
attitude 10, 20, 28, 49, 60, 64, 83, 84, 85, 86, 181, 193
autism 179
aviator 152

B

Basic Underwater Demolition 173
basketball 79, 177, 178, 179
Bates, Brooke 43
Bean, Alan 152
behavior 9, 12, 21, 29, 37, 39, 40, 43, 51, 52, 92, 99, 146, 169
beliefs 17, 20, 22, 42, 111, 142
Big Ben. *See* Roethlisberger, Ben
biofeedback 169
black hole 18, 19
BUD/s. *See* Basic Underwater Demolition
Bush, President George W. 178
butterfly 82, 186

C

California xx, xxi
cancer 99, 100
Christina Enevoldsen 39
Churchill, Winston 81, 127
CHZ. *See* circumstellar habitable zone
circumstellar habitable zone 50
clinical depression 46
cognitive 35, 133
cold weather survival 174
Collins, Jim 93
Colorado Springs 181
Columbus, Christopher 34
commitment 56, 57, 64, 112, 113, 115, 116, 117, 118, 119, 120, 121, 123, 126, 165, 172, 174, 181, 187
common cold 21, 122
conditioned defeat 48
Confucius 69
consistency of purpose 88
Csikszentmihalyi, Mihaly 180

D

Dark Side of the force 8
Darwin, Charles 62
Daurora, Jenifer 45
de Lint, Charles 68
developmental disability 179
diabetes 99
Disney, Walt 79
Disraeli, Ben 88
Dominican Republic 25

driving forces 9, 13, 14
Duquesne University 189

E

Earth 22, 33, 50, 57, 64
Eminem 80
Encyclopedia of Sport and Exercise Psychology 82, 192
End of the Ham 40
energy 18, 19, 23, 29, 30, 35, 84, 95, 96, 113, 117, 119, 121, 122, 147, 150, 151, 175
evolution 34, 43
executive team 49

F

Facebook 29, 56, 101, 171, 201
Famous Failures 79, 194
fear of failure 36, 98
fight or flight 33, 35
focus xxi, 14, 28, 38, 67, 102, 103, 112, 113, 128, 133, 138, 150, 151, 152, 153, 166, 175, 180, 181, 183
football 28, 81, 107, 165, 167, 179
Force Field Analysis 8, 9, 10, 11, 12, 13, 14, 15, 84, 88, 192, 194
fungi 21, 22, 192

G

Gemini 8 mission 152
Goldilocks zone.
   See circumstellar habitable zone
gold medal xx, xxi, 145

Goodyear, Charles 140
Gorbachev 8
gravitational pull 17, 20, 22
gravity 8, 17, 18, 19, 22, 23, 64, 66, 70, 88, 106, 179
gravity of life 8, 19, 22, 23, 64, 66, 70, 88

H

half empty 27, 28, 29, 30, 73
half full 27, 28, 29, 30, 73
Hamlet 141
Hayward, Nathaniel 140
heart disease 99
Hell Week 173
helplessness 36, 45, 47, 48, 194
homeostasis 49, 50, 51, 84
Honolulu, Hawaii xx

J

Jackson, Susan A. 180
Jedi Knight 8
J-Mac. *See* McElwain, Jason
Jobs, Steve 34, 80
Jordan. *See* Jordan, Michael
Jordan, Michael 61, 66, 79
Josephson, Michael 17
judo xvii, 100, 181
   black belt xviii, 181
   competition xviii, 3, 6, 56, 82, 100, 145
   national championship xviii, xx, 178, 196
   purple belt xviii
   San Diego, California xx

K

Kaizen 105
Keller, Helen 141, 165
Korean War 151

L

Land Warfare Training 174
La Romana 25
leadership 48, 181, 183, 187, 189
learned helplessness 45, 47
Lewin, Kurt 8, 88
Lincoln, Abraham 31, 80
Longfellow, Henry Wadsworth 20

M

Maier, Steve 45
Manning, Peyton 178
McChrystal, Stanley 185
McElwain, Jason 177, 179, 194
McGinnis, Elwood 43
McGinnis Sisters Special Food Stores 43, 44
memory 39, 123
mental imagery 160, 162
Mercury 50
Messi, Lionel 80
Mickey Mouse 79
Middle East 28
Moby Dick 58
monkey's knot 37
Multiverse 34

N

NASA 152
natural consequence 49
naval aviator 152
Navy SEALs 90, 105, 172, 174, 191
NBA championship 178
negative forces 9, 14, 88
negative self-talk 23
Nietzsche, Friedrich 165
Nobel Prize winner 79

O

obesity 10, 99
Obi-Wan Kenobi 8
Olympic athlete xxiii, 161
outcomes xxiii, 9
oxygen 30, 33, 48, 92

P

Pavlovian response 103
Peet's Coffee and Tea 58
Pennsylvania State University 189
performance xix, xx, xxii, 48, 49, 58, 59, 62, 70, 71, 72, 78, 88, 94, 100, 103, 111, 113, 146, 149, 157, 178, 179, 182
Pew internet study 101
Pittsburgh, Pennsylvania xxi, 43, 189
Pittsburgh Steelers 81
play to win 55
Porter, Phil 181, 191
positive 5, 9, 13, 14, 30, 63, 71, 83, 84, 85, 88, 100, 113, 121, 159, 160, 168
president of the United States 80, 179
primordial fear 32
public speaking 32
Punta Cana 25, 26

Q

Qi (energy) 149

R

Radcliffe College 141
Reagan, Ronald 8
restraining forces 9, 13, 14, 15
retardation of learning 46
Roethlisberger, Ben 81
Rohn, Jim 89, 118

S

San Antonio Spurs basketball team 178
SEAL. *See* Navy SEALs
SEAL Qualification Training 174
SEALs. *See* Navy SEALs
SEAL Team 173, 174
Seattle's Best 58
Seattle, Washington 57
self-efficacy 36
self-esteem 10, 12, 36, 48, 71, 145, 157
self-talk 23, 113, 121, 156, 157, 158, 159, 160, 162
Seligman, Martin 45
sensory pillow 46
SERE 174
Seth Godin 125
Shakespeare 141, 142
Shaolin master 149, 150
shuttle-box apparatus 45
Skywalker, Luke 8
social animals 32
social media 29, 101
Soviet Union 57
Space Race 57
Special Food Stores. *See* McGinnis Sisters Special Food Stores
Special Operations 172, 173
Star Wars 8, 57
success xxii, xxiii, 8, 22, 31, 36, 39, 44, 52, 55, 60, 61, 62, 66, 67, 68, 69, 70, 71, 73, 76, 78, 98, 99, 101, 106, 112, 113, 115, 116, 118, 120, 124, 126, 130, 131, 132, 135, 136, 145, 153, 159, 172, 187
Super Bowl 178
supernova 18, 19
supervisors 48, 49
Survival, Evasion, Resistance, and Escape. *See* SERE
survival of the fittest 63

T

tactical air operations 174
technology 34, 57, 70, 121, 123, 130
text messages 101, 129, 171
The Boy and the Butterfly 185
Thomas Edison 80, 111
Twitter 101, 201

U

United States military 172
University of Pennsylvania 45
U.S. Nationals xvii, xxi
USSR 57

V

Venus 50
viruses 21, 122
vision 21, 89, 116, 119, 121, 122, 128, 131, 132, 133,

161, 162, 163, 165, 166,
  168, 169
visualization 128
visual motor behavior rehearsal
  (VMBR) 169

W

Waitley, Denis 177
West Point 181
Wiersbe, Warren Wendel 107
Winfrey, Oprah 79
wrestling 86, 87, 88, 100, 105
Wright, Orville and Wilbur 34

X

X-15 152

Y

Yahoo 90, 194
yin and yang 8, 84

Z

zombie ant 21
zone xxii, 36, 50, 52, 113, 143,
  180, 182, 192

Also by David Loshelder

Protect Yourself: Top 10 Lifesaving Self-Defense Techniques

Contact information

For speaking engagements and interviews, please email Dave at: *Dave@takecareofnumberone.com.*

To order copies of: *Take Care of #1 So You Don't Step in #2* visit: *http://www.takecareofnumberone.com.*

Follow us on Facebook
https://www.facebook.com/TakeCareOfNo1
Follow us on Twitter
#TakeCareOfNo1

Mail to:
David Loshelder
P.O. Box 97910
Pittsburgh, PA 15227

www.ingramcontent.com/pod-product-compliance
Lightning Source LLC
Chambersburg PA
CBHW071701090426
42738CB00009B/1616